D0525057

Contents

Acknowledgements

I should like to thank all those who have helped prepare this second edition: the people whose positive responses to the first edition encouraged me that a second edition would be worthwhile; the teachers who welcomed me into their classrooms to watch them work, and whose creative efforts to help their pupils communicate appear here as examples.

I would particularly like to thank Sonya Gaynor, Leanne Masterson and Emma Brown for the photos which are new to this edition, and their parents, Sylvia and Frankie Gaynor; Helen and Mark Masterson, and Paula Brown for permission to include them; their teacher Ann Higgins, and Ms Catherine Whelan and the staff of the Developmental Day Centre, St Michael's House, Raheny where they are pupils; and Paul Murphy (senior audiovisual technician, St Patrick's College, Drumcondra) for his patience and expertise in taking these photos. Finally, thanks to Peter, who read and reread chapters and part chapters with the supportive but ever-critical eye of friendship.

Jean Ware
February 2003

Introduction to the Second Edition

About this book

This book is intended for all those working with people with profound and multiple learning difficulties (PMLD) whether as teachers or assistants in school, as instructors in social education centres, or as nurses or care staff in homes or hostels. The first edition was based on a research project funded by the ESRC which ran in two London schools. This second edition is also closely based on that research project, but also takes account of more recent research in the field, and of my own experience working with teachers in Britain and Ireland since the first edition was published.

When we use the term 'profound and multiple learning difficulties' to describe someone's disability, we mean that their degree of learning difficulty is so severe that they are functioning at a developmental level of two years or less (in practice, often well under a year) and also they have one or more other severe impairments, for example they may be unable to walk, be severely visually impaired, or both.

My intention in writing this book is to enable teachers and care staff, whether they are working with a group all of whom have PMLD or with individuals within a generally less severely disabled group, to create for their pupils or clients a particular type of interactive environment, which I call a responsive environment. I think that such environments are important for people with PMLD for several reasons. Firstly, they are positive environments for both pupils/clients and staff. Secondly, they capitalise on individual strengths which are often ignored, such as the differences in approach, tone of voice, etc. between staff members, and the different relationships that develop between staff and pupils/clients.

Thirdly, I also believe that a responsive environment can help children and adults with profound and multiple learning difficulties to make progress. I am not claiming that such progress will be dramatic. Nor am I claiming that providing a responsive environment is the only way progress can be obtained. Indeed I believe that the work of other researchers in the field also holds exciting prospects for enhancing learning opportunities and quality of life for people with PMLD. Examples include the work of Dunst in the States and Sheila Glenn and her colleagues in this country. There have been considerable advances in helping people with PMLD to communicate since the first edition of this book, such as the work of Coupe O'Kane and Goldbart on assessment and that of Grove and colleagues. The development of Picture Exchange Communication Systems (PECs) and alternative and augmentative communication more generally also offers exciting possibilities. However, I am convinced that a responsive environment must underpin all these other efforts.

Inevitably, because the project was carried out in schools, the examples refer to school-age children, but I hope that those who work in other settings will also find them relevant. Because this isn't always easy, in this second edition I have tried particularly to include illustrations of teachers working with teenagers. As with the first edition, teachers and support assistants working in schools will find few references to the National Curriculum because this book is not about curriculum content, but about the framework of interactions, whatever their content. That is not to say that the content of what is taught in schools or the activities that are provided for adults with PMLD or children outside school hours are not important, simply that these are areas this book does not attempt to cover. Since the first edition of this book was published, we (Christina Tilstone, Richard Byers, Michael Thompson and myself) have had the opportunity to work with groups of teachers on these curriculum issues, through a QCA-funded project. This work has been published by QCA as *Curriculum guidelines for pupils with learning difficulties* (QCA/DfEE 2001) which I believe should help those working in schools to address curriculum issues in a way that also promotes a responsive environment.

The first chapter outlines what a responsive environment is and the research that supports our view that it is an appropriate environment for people with PMLD. The next four chapters each look at one aspect of the responsive environment for people with PMLD and are intended to be 'done' rather than simply read. Chapter 6, which deals with how a responsive environment can be used to develop and extend the communication skills of people with PMLD beyond their earliest beginnings now also incorporates a new section on how a responsive environment can be created in inclusive settings. Chapter 7, new to this edition, looks at how technology can be used to extend the responsive environment. The final chapter is concerned with how, once you've created a responsive environment in your school or centre, you can help it to last.

'Doing' the book

Ideally each chapter should be worked through at a meeting or meetings between all the relevant staff, because an important aspect of creating a responsive environment is the sharing of information between staff – it really doesn't matter if you've only got half an hour at lunch-times every couple of weeks – this book is designed to be used in situations like that. It isn't a good idea to try and cover several chapters in a longer session such as an INSET day, because it's important that you get the chance to try out the ideas one at a time, and get familiar with each one before you attempt the next one.

One person will need to agree to be the coordinator. It could be the teacher responsible for pupils with PMLD; it might in some schools be the speech and language therapist, since communication is a central aspect of a responsive environment; in a small residential home, it could be the person in charge, or it might be the psychologist if one is available to help. The coordinator is responsible for making sure that all the materials needed for a particular session are available, for leading the session, and for giving other staff positive feedback when they try out the ideas suggested. If you decide to implement a responsive environment on a long-term basis the coordinator will also need to monitor it and continue giving other staff positive feedback about the way they are working.

By all the relevant staff I mean all those who contribute to the interactive environment for the pupils you are concerned with. So if, for example, you run a class specifically for pupils with PMLD, you would want to have present: yourself, all the assistants who work with you, the physio and speech therapist and the school nurse, if any of these people interact regularly with the pupils. You would also want any other staff who work regularly with your class to be present if at all possible – perhaps they have a session with the music teacher while you take her class for PE – if possible she should come to the sessions where you work through this book. Obviously, this is a counsel of perfection, but it is important that all the regular classroom staff should be present if at all possible, even if that means having to make arrangements for someone else to look after the pupils for half an hour or so. If you work in a residential care establishment, it would mean getting together all the staff who have regular contact with the people you are concerned with on the various shifts. Potentially, unless the service in which you work is structured to allow that to happen, that could be very difficult, and you might have to have two groups going through the book separately.

Of course, I'm not suggesting that this book isn't worth reading unless you can take part in such a group. I hope that however you use it, it will enhance your work with people with PMLD and so make a positive contribution to their lives.

Jean Ware
January 2003

CHAPTER 1

The Importance of a Responsive Environment

Introduction

This chapter is a little different from those that follow because it gives basic information about what a responsive environment is, and looks at the evidence for suggesting that such an environment can be beneficial to people with PMLD and the staff who work with them.

> If you are coordinating a group working through the book together, you need to read this chapter before your group meeting, so that you can lead a discussion based on the summary at the end.

What is 'a responsive environment'?

By 'a responsive environment', I mean an environment in which people get responses to their actions, get the opportunity to give responses to the actions of others, and have an opportunity to take the lead in interaction. There are two ways in which people receive responses to their actions: from other people, and from seeing things happen as a result of what they do. This may sound rather abstract, but some examples should clarify what I mean.

If you speak to a friend, they will probably respond in some way, perhaps by pausing in what they are doing, or by looking at you, or by replying; indicating that they are attending to you. What is more, you behave as if you expect a response from them, pausing after your initial greeting to give them chance to reply. If there is no apparent response, you are likely to repeat your greeting, perhaps more loudly.

If you see a colleague approaching a closed door with an armful of equipment and you move to open it for them, they will probably acknowledge your action in some way, perhaps by smiling or by thanking you.

When you turn on the tap, water comes out (unless of course the mains have been switched off). You press the emergency button in your classroom because a child is having a severe seizure and the nurse and head teacher come running.

Similarly, a young infant may start cooing, and attract a response from a nearby adult, they may hear a familiar voice and vocalise; attracting a greeting from the adult in response. The same child may hear the noises of preparation as a drink is being made, and smile in anticipation, again attracting a response from the person who is making the drink. They may hit the mobile attached over their cot, and the toy reacts by moving and making noises. In other words, their actions receive responses.

At another time the child may be lying quiet but alert in their pram, and be asked by a passing adult: 'What are you thinking about, Joe?' The adult who asks the question, although they are not expecting a verbal reply, pauses in much the same way as if they had been addressing another adult. There is an expectation that the infant will respond, perhaps just by smiling or maybe by cooing; and this may well lead to the conversation being continued. To the smile the adult says: 'It's a secret is it?' and so on.

When you have a discussion with a friend the initiative passes backwards and forwards between you, so that overall neither you nor they dominate the conversation. Perhaps you start the topic – holidays for example; but then they raise the issue of whether you are going to go self-catering or think about a hotel or guesthouse; you raise the possibility of going out of season, they suggest taking others along; you are equal participants in the dialogue. Like conversations, joint activities are most satisfying for both partners when first one takes the lead and then the other. Of course there are exceptions, as when one person has a much higher level of expertise in the activity than the other, this person may dominate that particular activity. In the same way, when an infant and caregiver are playing together, first one and then the other takes the lead, perhaps mum gives the child a toy to play with, and comments as the child examines it. After a few minutes the child's eye is caught by the sun's light reflected in some shiny paper, she vocalises excitedly and this then becomes the focus of mum's attention as well as the child's. When an infant is very young, or the activity is a novel one, the caregiver may dominate the interaction, but as the infant gets older and more skilful he or she quickly becomes an equal partner in the interaction, sometimes being the leader and sometimes following the caregiver's lead. At one level then, there's nothing very extraordinary about a responsive environment. It's part of the normal experience of most people from birth to adulthood, and particularly of normal, healthy infants in interaction with their mothers (or whoever happens to be their main caregiver). Research on such early interactions shows that, long before the infant has any intention to communicate (in the sense of acting with a deliberate intention to affect someone else's behaviour), adults treat him or her as if their actions had meaning. The example of the adult's response to the alert but quiet baby given above is an example of such behaviour.

Why is a responsive environment important?

So, if a responsive environment is unremarkable, why is it important? It is important because :

- Babies learn to communicate by being treated as if their actions had meaning in other words by others responding to them as if they had something important to say.
- Infants who experience a responsive environment engage in more social interaction and develop into social beings more quickly.
- They also learn more quickly.

I think that a responsive environment is also very important for another reason. It embodies the respect and dignity with which all people, whatever their age, abilities or disabilities, ought to be treated. So, even if we couldn't demonstrate that it made any difference at all in terms of learning or progress, it would still be important for that reason alone.

How do we know? Some evidence from research

On the positive side: evidence from research suggests that it's by being treated as if they were really trying to say something important that babies learn to communicate (e.g. Snow, Dubber and de Blauw 1982; Snow 1984; Scoville 1984). They also make faster social and cognitive progress. For example, Lewis and Coates (1980) found an association between mothers' responsiveness and the cognitive development of their 12-week-old infants, and report that similar associations have been found by other researchers. Of course, such an association does not prove that the mother's responsiveness causes the infant's cognitive gains. It might be that mothers are more responsive to infants who are cognitively advanced.

However, a study by Anderson and Sawin (1983) showed that a simple intervention procedure designed to help mothers become familiar with what their babies could do (having the mother present while a neonatal behaviour assessment was administered and explained) was successful in increasing mothers' responsiveness to their (non-disabled) infants. The infants' responsiveness to their mothers also increased, and they were also more alert and showed more positive affect than infants whose mothers had not received the intervention, although they were only one month old. Anderson and Sawin suggest that the only possible explanation for this change in the infant's behaviour was that it resulted from the mother's increased awareness of how to respond to her infant. In another study of typically developing infants, which followed mother-infant pairs for two years after a brief intervention based on the same neonatal assessment, the researchers not only showed mothers what their babies could do, but how they could encourage these behaviours (Gomes-Pedro *et al.* 1995). This study found that better interactive patterns in the experimental group persisted across the two years.

On the negative side, much of the evidence for the importance of a responsive environment comes from research that compares the progress of infants who experience more and less responsive environments during the early months and years of life. Of course, not all infants experience an equally responsive environment. For example, the infant may be separated from his or her main caregiver through illness. In one study of such babies, Minde *et al.* (1983) found that mothers of babies who were seriously ill at birth interacted with them less even after they had recovered and gone home, than mothers of babies who had also been in the neonatal intensive care unit, but who hadn't been so seriously ill. The caregiver may be also be less able to respond to their baby for a variety of reasons, for example they may be stressed or unwell.

Research with typically developing infants also suggests that (at least in the laboratory) when babies don't get responses to what they do they may find it harder to learn, become less active and show less enjoyment. For example, when Watson and Ramey gave two-month-olds the chance to control the movement of a mobile by kicking, those who had previously seen the mobile repeatedly without being able to control it failed to learn (Watson and Ramey 1972). In a more recent study of infants aged from three to four months, O'Brien found that when they were presented with a mobile which they had previously been able to work for themselves, but which was now operated independently of anything they did, they smiled less and fussed more (O'Brien 1991).

Do people with PMLD experience a responsive environment?

If then a responsive environment is important for social, communicative and intellectual development, the extent to which such an environment is experienced by people with PMLD is clearly of interest. Furthermore, since people with PMLD may well remain in the pre-intentional stages of communication for many years, such an environment may continue to be important for them at school or even later in life.

When I first started looking at what was happening in classrooms for pupils with PMLD, I found that on the whole they had few opportunities for interaction of any sort, and even fewer that gave them the opportunity to participate (Ware and Evans 1986; Ware 1987). In another observational study of classrooms carried out around the same time as my initial work, Houghton *et al.* (1987) found that students with severe disabilities received only very few responses to their initiations expressing choices.

This was similar to the situation in residential institutions reported earlier by other researchers (e.g. Paton and Stirling 1974; Veit, Allen and Chinsky 1976). Of course, this research is rather old, and maybe things have changed for the better in the last 25 years; especially as staff: resident ratios are likely to have improved and people with learning difficulties have moved into smaller community homes. Regrettably, however, an extensive trawl through the literature for the second edition of this book produced many more recent examples of the same situation (e.g. Golden and Reese 1996). One recent study found that both the quality and quantity of staff resident interactions were related to the severity of residents' disability (Seys *et al.* 1998). Even in a very recent study by Realon *et al.* (2002), adults with profound disabilities were only engaged in interactions with staff for an average of ten per cent of the time, and for some individuals within the group this was as low as two per cent. Felce (1998) suggests that this apparent lack of progress reflects the fact that small homelike environments are not by themselves sufficient to ensure that people with severe and profound intellectual disabilities experience high quality interactions.

Perhaps, though, this lack of opportunity for interaction is a result of being in a segregated environment, where your peers are as unskilled at interacting as you are, and people with PMLD fare better in inclusive settings. Unfortunately, there is now a growing volume of research which suggests that pupils with PMLD often have little opportunity to experience positive/contingency-sensitive interactions with their peers in inclusive schools (see Chapter 6).

What sort of interactive environment do infants with disabilities have?

By contrast, non-disabled young children functioning at a similar developmental level are active participants in interactions with their caregivers, and this active participation is regarded as important for their development (see above). It would be useful, therefore, to know whether infants with PMLD also participate actively in early interactions with their caregivers.

Unfortunately, there is very little research that examines the interactive environments experienced by infants with PMLD. The one or two studies that have been published suggest that the interactive environments experienced by infants with severe disabilities are significantly different from those of infants without such difficulties. One notable example is a study by Campbell *et al.* (1989) of infants for whom serious delivery problems had meant that they were starved of oxygen around the time of birth. Campbell *et al.* found that even in the early days after infants were first discharged from hospital there were differences in interactions between mothers and infants who eventually developed a severe disability such as cerebral palsy and those who did not.

There are many more studies that compare the interactive environments of groups of infants with a variety of different disabilities with that of non-disabled infants. Looking at these studies, in addition to the few that deal specifically with infants with PMLD, can help us to predict the sort of interactive environment likely to be experienced by infants who have PMLD.

Dichtelmiller (1995) found differences in interaction patterns between mothers and their infants with very low birth weights and moderate to severe disabilities and mothers and their infants who had very low birth weights but without noticeable disabilities. Furthermore the interaction patterns of the mothers whose very low birth weight infants did not have disabilities were very similar to those of a comparison group of mothers and full-term babies. Dichtelmiller also found a significant relationship between interaction patterns and cognitive development between the ages of one and three.

Barrera, Rosenbaum and Cunningham (1987) also conducted a longitudinal study which compared very low birth weight infants and full-term infants between the ages of 4 and 16 months. They found that the very low birth weight infants were more passive and less intense, scored lower on developmental tests and generally experienced a less stimulating and responsive home environment than the full-term infants. In another study, Barrera and Vella (1987) found that infants with physical disabilities made less eye contact with their mothers than normal infants and that their mothers engaged in less physical interaction and more commanding and verbal behaviour.

Field (1983) found that four-month-old pre-term infants observed in spontaneous play interaction with their mothers spent more time crying and less time vocalising than 'normal' infants. They were also less likely to smile and/or vocalise in response to their mothers, less likely to look happy and more likely to look sad. Likewise their mothers were more likely to look sad, and less likely to look happy than the mothers of the 'normal' infants. Additionally, they vocalised more, and Field suggests that this represents their attempts to get responses from an unresponsive baby. However the pre-term babies spent more time than the 'normal' infants with their gaze averted from their mothers, in other words it looked as if the mothers' additional efforts were counterproductive.

Similarly, Hanzlik and Stevenson (1986) found that mothers of infants with both cerebral palsy and learning difficulties demonstrated a higher overall level of behaviour, and a higher level of commands than mothers of non-disabled infants of either the same chronological age (CA) (mean 21 months) or the same mental age (MA) (mean 11.6 months). The cerebral palsied infants, and another group of infants with moderate learning difficulties (but not cerebral palsy), like those in Field's study had a lower overall level of behaviour than non-disabled infants of the same chronological age, and they also engaged in fewer verbal interactions with their mothers. Furthermore Hanzlik and Stevenson found that both the infants with cerebral palsy and learning difficulties and the infants with learning difficulties alone were more likely to be involved in competing behaviour with their mothers than non-disabled infants of either the same CA or the same MA.

Like Field, and Hanzlik and Stevenson, Mahoney and Robenalt (1986) compared the interactions of infants with and without disabilities with their mothers during free play. They found that the infants with Down's syndrome in their study (who had MAs of 15–19 months) 'were less active communicative partners' than a carefully matched group without disabilities. They also found that the mothers of the children with Down's syndrome were more likely to dominate the interaction rather than mother and infant being more or less equal partners, as was the case with the non-disabled group. That is, the mothers of the Down's syndrome infants took more turns, gave more commands, and spent less time responding to their children than the mothers of the non-disabled group.

A number of other researchers working with children with a variety of disabilities and their caregivers have similarly found that the caregivers tend to dominate interactions. Studies by Barrera, Watson and Adelstein (1987) and by Garrad (1986) are particularly interesting. Barrera et al. compared interactions between mothers and their infants with Down's syndrome with those of mothers and their non-disabled infants at three months and two years. They found that while mothers of the non-disabled infants became more responsive over time, this was not true for the mothers of the infants with Down's syndrome. Garrad looked at how interactions developed as the children got older. She found that mothers used more controlling questions with developmentally delayed than with non-delayed children; and, as the children got older this difference increased, since mothers tended to use even more controlling questions with children with developmental delays and fewer with non-delayed children. Another study by Hanzlik (1990), of infants with cerebral palsy and developmental delay also found that mothers of these infants were more directive and less positive in their interactions than mothers of non-disabled infants.

Mahoney and Robenalt, like Field, think that it is likely that this increased use of commands by mothers of disabled children results from their attempts to elicit a greater amount of activity from their child by asking them to do things; but that this could well result in the child becoming even less active. Zirpoli and Bell (1987) suggest that a vicious circle may develop in which early high levels of caregiver behaviour may decrease as the child appears to be unresponsive to their attempts.

Bray (1988) compared children with Down's syndrome and severe learning difficulties aged between two and six years with two groups of non-disabled children (same chronological age and same mental age). She found that the children with Down's syndrome were less likely to be involved in interactions where they took the lead, or where the lead was equally shared between the partners, than children of the same chronological age. They were also less likely to experience equal interactions than children of the same mental age. Bray also found that the Down's syndrome group were more likely to be involved in negative interactions and suggested that non-disabled children may stimulate their parents into appropriate forms of interaction whereas disabled children may not.

Although none of this research involves infants with PMLD, there is some evidence that the more severely disabled an infant is, the more acute these problems are likely to be. For example, Terdal *et al.* (1976) and Cunningham *et al.* (1981) found that children with more severe learning difficulties were less likely to respond adequately to mothers' initiations than those with less severe difficulties.

These research studies provide a good deal of evidence that parents and other caregivers find it more difficult to respond to children with disabilities than to non-disabled children, and are more likely to experience negative or unsatisfying interactions with them. Consequently infants with disabilities of all kinds are less likely to experience a responsive environment than non-disabled infants. Or perhaps we should say that they experience a less responsive environment than non-disabled infants.

Why not?

Why might this be? It could simply be because the adult knows that the infant has been labelled 'disabled' and responds accordingly and in some cases this may contribute to the caregiver's problems. However, this seems unlikely to be the main problem, particularly in the light of research like that of Campbell *et al.* (see above). Campbell and her colleagues found that differences in interaction between mother-infant pairs where the infant had a significant degree of disability and those where the infant did not preceded the diagnosis. And, if we return to our earlier example, we can see that for people with PMLD the natural experience of a responsive environment may be difficult for a number of reasons.

For instance, hearing the voice of a familiar adult saying their name, the child with PMLD may vocalise, like the non-disabled infant, but they might equally well relax slightly; a response not easily noticed and so less likely to lead the adult to continue interacting with them. Hearing the drinks being prepared, they might move their lips and tongue rather than smile. This movement might not so easily be connected with the drinks preparation, and so again might not be noted and commented on by the adult. Indeed, several investigators have noticed that both caregivers and staff such as teachers are less likely to respond to unconventional behaviours (such as tongue thrusts, eye blinks and shifts in position) as communication than they are to behaviours such as vocalisations (e.g. Downing and Seigel-Causey 1988).

A child with PMLD may not vocalise as frequently as a non-disabled child, and even if by doing so they attract the attention of an adult who responds, they may not respond to the adult's conversation attempt immediately, or in the way the adult expects and, consequently, the adult is discouraged from continuing the interaction, or even from responding to the child on a subsequent occasion.

When we examine interactions with the environment, the situation may be even more problematic. A child with PMLD might be provided with a switch-operated toy to compensate for the motor impairments which make it very difficult for them to work mobiles etc. They may move an arm, activating the switch and turn on the toy, which reacts with noises, lights and movement. Attempting to repeat the movement they may fail to activate the switch for several reasons: perhaps their movements are uncoordinated and they do not make contact with the switch pad, perhaps (due to the motor impairment) the effort of the first attempt has tired them, and they do not press hard enough, and so again the toy is not activated. Or there may be mechanical or electrical faults which again result in the toy failing to respond – another child may inadvertently have pulled out the leads, the batteries may be flat or the contacts dirty.

Research evidence backs the view that people with PMLD do have some characteristics that make interacting with them more difficult and potentially less satisfying for the other person. For example they may 'behave' very slowly. Young infants have a natural behavioural rhythm – they do something for a few seconds (cooing, kicking their legs, etc.) and then pause. Adults interact with them by waiting for the pause and then inserting a response, cooing back, talking to the infant, etc., and then pausing themselves, giving the infant an opportunity to respond again. In this way the basic turn-taking of conversation begins. A child with PMLD may produce very few behaviours with very long pauses in between, so that it's difficult for the other person to get a feel for the rhythm; or there may indeed be little rhythm – a particular behaviour may at times be almost continuous with no pauses for an interacting partner to use.

Additionally it's possible that it is more difficult to tell what infants with PMLD feel from the way they behave (their vocalisations, facial expressions and so on). We know from research with infants with a variety of disabilities, for example visual or hearing impairment, that the meaning of their behaviours, may be difficult to interpret even for those who know them well (Dunst 1985). Reviewing recent research on this topic, Spiker, Boyce and Boyce (2002) conclude that the signals and cues of children with disabilities are less consistent and predictable than those of typically developing children and that, in turn, the parent may have more difficulty in reading them and engaging responsively. Yoder (1987) demonstrated that for infants with learning difficulties and/or physical disabilities the difficulty in interpreting cues is greater for those with more severe disabilities. This can make interacting quite unsatisfying or even stressful for the caregiver, who gets little positive feedback. Since this difficulty occurs for adults interacting both with infants who have sensory impairments and those who have learning difficulties or physical disabilities it seems very unlikely not to be the case for those who have a combination of some or all of these disabilities.

Wilcox *et al.* (1990) examined the extent to which different adults (mothers, teachers, speech therapists) recognised communicative cues from children with developmental disabilities. They found that there were quite enormous differences between individuals; but over and above this they suggest that there may be factors specific to child-adult pairs that lead to some children receiving inconsistent responses to their communication attempts. Goldberg (1977) suggests that an infant's readability, responsiveness and predictability are all important in letting parents know that their behaviour is effective (and thus encouraging them to continue interacting).

An experiment by Murray and Trevarthen (1986) with non-disabled infants demonstrates just how important the infant's responses are in maintaining a satisfying interaction. Murray and Trevarthen asked mothers to talk to their infants via a video link. When the conversation was 'live', mothers and infants responded to each other just as they would have done when interacting naturally. When mothers were played a recording of their infant but still believed they were in touch with them through the video link, they became conscious that the infant was not responding to them and their talk contained more commands and negatives. As Murray and Trevarthen point out, the mothers' behaviour in the recorded situation resembles that of caregivers in interaction with disabled infants. (Although the information obtained by this experiment is very interesting it is, to say the least, ethically dubious to obtain it by deceiving the mothers, as appears to have been the case.)

Perhaps though, this difference between the environment normally experienced by non-disabled young infants and that provided (both at home and at school) for those with PMLD is an appropriate adaptation to their particular difficulties. Although a few writers suggest that this is indeed the case, the balance of the evidence from research is that the way adults (parents, caregivers, school staff) often adapt to people with PMLD is not in the interests of their social and cognitive development.

Can we do anything about it?

If then a responsive environment is important to the development of social, communicative and cognitive skills, is there anything we can do to overcome the problems experienced in interacting with people with PMLD in order to provide them with the type of interactive environment likely to facilitate their development?

In the next section I examine the evidence that it is possible to change interactive environments, looking at each of the three aspects in turn, and then go on to consider the implications for those who work with people with PMLD. Not all the research addresses all aspects of a responsive environment, and much of it is concerned either with infants or children without any sort of disability, or, like that concerning differences in caregiver-infant interaction between disabled and non-disabled infants, with those whose disabilities are less severe than those this book is concerned with. Nevertheless it's this evidence that provides pointers to the sorts of investigation it would be useful to carry out with people with PMLD, and it's also this type of evidence that underlies the research project on which this book is based.

Getting responses to one's actions

Anderson and Sawin's study with non-disabled infants (mentioned above) showed that it was possible to make mothers more responsive to their infants by means of a simple intervention procedure, and that this resulted in infants being more responsive, alert and positive. Letourneau (1999), in a pilot study of teenage mothers and their babies, found that an intervention designed to improve the quality of interactions was successful both in increasing the extent to which interactions were contingently responsive and in enhancing the infants' cognitive development.

McCollum (1984) worked with caregiver-infant pairs for whom social interaction had been identified as a problem area. She demonstrates that an individualised intervention, the Social Interaction Assessment and Intervention, enabled caregivers to adjust their interactions in the direction of greater responsiveness. The change in caregiver behaviour resulted not only in increased infant participation in the interaction, but also in greater enjoyment for both partners. This positive effect was true for infant-caregiver pairs with a wide variety of reasons for their social interaction difficulties, including at least one with severe cerebral palsy.

Barrera, Rosenbaum and Cunningham (1986) conducted a particularly interesting study with pre-term babies and their parents. Their study compared two forms of intervention, one aimed mainly at parent-infant interaction, and the other aimed primarily at the infants' cognitive development, and two non-intervention groups, one of pre-term and one of full-term infants. They found that both intervention groups made gains in cognitive development during the period of the study compared with the non-intervention group of pre-term infants, and that by the end of the study differences between the pre-term intervention groups and the full-term group had disappeared. Of particular interest is their finding that the group who had the parent-infant intervention most closely resembled the full-term group in the high levels of responsiveness of mothers to their infants, and in the extent to which they provided a variety of stimulation. Barrera *et al.* (1986) suggest that the parent-infant intervention effectively 'normalises' the home environment. Like Bray (above) they suggest that, while normal healthy infants may stimulate their parents into providing experiences that foster development, the parents of infants with disabilities may need help to do so.

Opportunities to respond to the actions of others

Waiting for the child to respond is a critical feature of a responsive environment. Unfortunately, because a child with PMLD may respond very slowly, or not all, or in an unexpected way, there is a tendency for adults to behave as if they are not expecting a response. MacDonald and Gillette (1984) say that caregivers and teachers are often surprised when they do wait for the child to take a turn, at what he or she is able to do. They also point out the need to wait in a way that suggests that a response is expected. In the Contingency-Sensitive Environments Project, we found that children were more likely to respond when the adult was looking attentively at the child while she waited.

Opportunities to take the lead in interactions

Turn-taking (waiting for the child to act first, imitating the child's behaviour, following the child's lead) was a major feature of an intervention used by Mahoney and Powell (1988) with parents and their moderately or severely disabled infants. They found that parents were, in general, very successful at implementing these strategies. Furthermore, implementation was associated with an increase in the responsiveness of the interactive environment the parents provided for their children, and with greater developmental gains for the children. However, for some parents there also seemed to be a negative effect in important areas such as warmth and enjoyment.

A study by Hauser-Cram (1993), which looked at interactive skills in general, found that the children of mothers who became much more skilled at interacting with their disabled children during the course of early intervention projects, made considerable progress in their cognitive and social development. One year into this study, it was not possible for the investigators to identify any differences between these mothers and their children and others for whom these large increases did not occur. They suggest this lack of difference between those who did and those who did not show major improvement is positive, suggesting that caregiver and child characteristics are not crucial factors in improving interactions. However there may have been important differences in delivery of the intervention to these mothers and children, which were not examined in this study.

What about interventions with staff in settings for adults with PMLD?

All these studies involve interactions between caregivers and their young children. Since the first edition of this book was published, there have been a number of attempts to change the interactions of staff working with adults with PMLD. Unfortunately, these often seem to have less dramatic results. For example, Golden and Reese (1996) found that training only increased positive staff interactions slightly. Furthermore, these were not accompanied by positive changes in resident behaviours. This study highlights the potential difficulties in attempting to provide people with PMLD with a responsive environment in schools or other group environments.

Nind *et al.* (2001) analysed videos made by teacher volunteers of their attempts at engaging pupils ranging from three to 19 years in interaction following training in Intensive Interaction. They found that although all the teachers did adapt their interactions in response to individual pupils, they used only a limited number of the interaction strategies suggested in training and were not necessarily successful in engaging their pupils. However, where pupils were successfully engaged, teachers were using a wider range of strategies adapted from caregiver-infant interactions. This study is important because it supports my view that interactions based on those that caregivers use naturally with young infants are appropriate in working with older individuals with PMLD.

Other important aspects of a responsive environment

The possibility of accelerating cognitive and social development is not, however, the only reason why I see it as important to provide a responsive environment for people with PMLD. For example, Favell *et al.* (1996) suggest that relatively simple interventions in interaction can increase the happiness of at least some individuals with PMLD. They argue that clients' happiness should receive a higher priority in services for people with learning difficulties. At the most fundamental level a responsive environment is important because it is through our interactions with others that we learn who we are. The educational philosopher Aspin argues that it is this principle that underlies the whole special educational enterprise (Aspin 1982). His argument is similar to that of the communication experts I examined earlier, that it is by being treated as communicators that we learn to communicate, but more comprehensive. He suggests that it is by interaction with other persons that we learn to become persons. It is not necessary to follow the philosophical logic involved in this argument to grasp the essential point that is being made, that interaction is important for personal development. As Aspin points out, this is at root a moral argument. In the end I am saying that it is important to provide people with PMLD with a responsive environment, because experiencing this sort of interactive environment teaches us that we are valued and respected.

There is a third and more pragmatic reason why I see a responsive environment as important: that is its impact on staff who work with people with PMLD. Classroom staff involved in the Contingency-Sensitive Environments Project reported increased enjoyment and satisfaction with their work. They generally put this down to their increased awareness of the children's responses. Like the caregivers of infants with disabilities, they found interactions with children who seemed not to respond positively stressful and unsatisfying; conversely they derived satisfaction and enjoyment from positive interactions with pupils.

Summary and overview

The research reviewed in this chapter shows that there are subtle but important differences in the interactions with caregivers experienced by babies and infants with and without handicaps.

In summary: babies and infants with all kinds of disabilities and particularly those who have learning difficulties are likely to have interactions with their caregivers in which:

- they are rather passive partners;
- they get comparatively few responses from their caregivers;
- the caregiver is the dominant partner;
- there are clashes between the infant and the caregiver (i.e. both are 'speaking' at once).

Consequently, and very importantly, such interactions may well be less enjoyable for both infant and caregiver than those between a non-disabled infant and their caregiver. Although little of this research involves infants with PMLD, there is every reason to believe that they will experience the same problems in interactions as those with less severe difficulties.

It is clear, however, that a number of researchers have been successful in enabling caregivers (usually mothers) to alter their interactions in such a way as to create a more responsive environment for their infant, and that, in general, this has resulted not only in the infant themselves becoming more responsive, but in the interactions being more enjoyable and satisfying for the mother. There is also some evidence of a positive impact on cognitive and social development. However, all these studies (not surprisingly) have involved 1:1 interactions of an extended nature.

Most of the interactions experienced by pupils with PMLD within a school context are not like this. For example, Goldbart (1980) and Ware (1987) both found that over 50 per cent of interactions in PMLD classes lasted less than one minute. Even where an adult is working with a pupil for a more extended period, it may well be that the main focus is not on the interaction itself, but on for example the completion of a physiotherapy or skills programme. Is it possible for staff to create a responsive environment under these conditions?

What little research there is on the interactions between adults and young children in groups suggests that it is more difficult for adults to maintain a responsive environment when they have responsibility for more than one child. For example, Schaffer and Liddell (1984) found that nursery nurses were more likely to ignore children's initiations, and were more controlling when they were responsible for four children than in a 1:1 situation.

It seems, then, that if you are a member of staff involved with a *group* of people with PMLD the odds are stacked against you in terms of having interactions with them that are responsive, and enjoyable and satisfying for you and them. Nonetheless, in the Contingency-Sensitive Environments Project we found that staff were able to create a responsive environment in their classrooms, without any increase in staff ratios, and without detriment to the activities they felt it was important for them to carry out with the children.

The rest of this book is about how that was done, and how you can adapt the strategies we found successful to your own situation.

CHAPTER 2

Getting Started, Making Sense of Children's Behaviour

Introduction

The research that I reviewed in Chapter 1 suggests that the difficulties we may have in telling how a person with PMLD feels from their facial expressions and behaviour (readability) and in engaging in turn-taking with them (synchronicity) may be at least partly responsible for the difficulty we often have in attributing meaning to their behaviour. Yet we know that we learn to communicate by being treated as communicators, and that it is being able to attribute meaning to our behaviour that enables others to treat us as communicators. If we are going to help people with PMLD become communicators, therefore, it is vital that we learn to make sense of their behaviour.

Anyone who has worked or lived with an individual with PMLD over a period of time probably already knows a great deal about their behaviour and what it means. However, we can sometimes be very unsure about how to interpret particular behaviours; and we may not always be aware of all the available information in making our judgements about their meaning.

As I mentioned in Chapter 1, there are a number of potential differences between the behaviour of someone with PMLD and a young infant without disabilities which contribute to this problem. For example, someone may have a disability such as cerebral palsy which makes their movements jerky and uncoordinated, and therefore more difficult to interpret. They may very well take much longer than other people to make any response, and this can hinder our attempts to link their responses with particular events or lead us to conclude that they are not going to respond at all and perhaps abandon the interaction. They may have a severe visual impairment, and like young infants with such an impairment be unlikely to make eye contact, making us unsure whether or not they are attending. Or, as suggested by Fraiberg (1977) in relation to blind babies, they may move their hands when another child's response would be a change of facial expression. In addition, there are the other problems I have already discussed such as apparently continuous behaviour which allows you no space in which to respond.

Another problem, particularly with older people with PMLD, may be the discrepancy between their level of functioning and their appearance. It's difficult (quite aside from issues of age-appropriateness) to interact with someone who is physically a teenager in a manner comparable to that we would use with a newish baby, yet the young person with PMLD may well be functioning at a similar level in many ways. This list of potential difficulties may seem very daunting; however, bearing them in mind may help you in your efforts to understand what an individual is 'saying' through their behaviour. Perhaps though, the greatest problem lies in the next step – using information about the meaning of behaviours to develop the communication skills of the individual.

Communicative intent

One approach that may be helpful in this regard is to look at the work on the development of intentional communication, of which there has been a good deal in recent years (see Coupe O'Kane and Goldbart 1998 for a review). Although this development is actually continuous, many authors identify three important stages (see Table 2.1).

Stage 1

At first, the behaviours that adults use as signals of the baby's needs are involuntary responses to internal or external stimuli (for example startling to a loud noise, crying when hungry or screaming in pain). However, at a very early stage of development infants also engage in voluntary behaviour such as waving their arms and legs. Adults act as if the infant is trying to communicate through these behaviours; for example increased arm and leg activity may be interpreted as excitement about some impending event – 'Yes, we're going to the park very soon.'

Stage 2

Next, according to these researchers, the infant gradually begins to act purposefully, reaching out in order to pick up a toy, crawling across the room towards mum, or the sunlight streaming through the window.

Stage 3

Finally, the infant reaches the stage where they point to the toy out of reach on the shelf, and look at mum as if to say, 'Please get that for me.' This development is almost certainly assisted by adults interpreting purposeful behaviours as attempts to communicate, so that when a child reaches for a toy that is out of reach the adult intervenes, saying, 'Oh, do you want me to get you the fire-engine?'

Table 2.1 Stages of development of intentional communication

1. Voluntary behaviour: e.g. arm movements, leg movements, apparently random vocalisations which do not seem to be connected to environmental events in any way, but are voluntary in the sense that they are under the individual's control rather than occurring as the result of, for example, a muscular spasm.
2. Purposeful behaviour: e.g. playing with a toy, walking deliberately towards something, picking up a piece of equipment.
3. Intentional communication: the child acts deliberately and spontaneously to attract someone else's attention: e.g. a child may reach out and touch you, look at you and smile or may initiate eye contact. They may vocalise when you have just left them to deal with someone else.

This sequence, however, emphasises one aspect of communication, communication in order to achieve a goal. Much communication is not of this type, but is participated in for its own sake. Furthermore the steps between the stages are extremely large for people who may be in the pre-intentional stages of communication for many years. In the Contingency-Sensitive Environments Project we identified another way in which behaviour develops from the first (voluntary behaviour) stage which we called 'Responses to the environment'. This includes behaviours such as looking up when someone passes nearby, or when the door squeaks, or smiling and looking when the wind waves the leaves of a tree just outside the window. 'Responses to the environment' also include responses to other people who are not actually interacting with the individual concerned; such as vocalising when another child/client vocalises, or in response to a particular member of staff speaking to another person.

Especially for pupils with profound motor impairments, who may rarely be able to demonstrate purposeful behaviour (at least without the aid of technology), this provides an alternative opportunity for adults to intervene in a way that will assist the development of communication. It also highlights the importance of developing social interaction, as well as communication to achieve a goal. For example, when a child vocalises in response to the voice of a familiar visitor, the adult might say: 'Yes, that's Mary come to see us, do you want to talk to her?'

In the first edition of this book I said that it is not really clear where this type of behaviour fits into the sequence except that, like purposeful behaviour, it is nearer intentional communication than behaviour that is merely voluntary. Coupe O'Kane and Goldbart (1998) have since suggested that it is less developmentally advanced than purposeful behaviour and can be recognised as a stage in the development of communication in 'normal' infants. However, I think it is still useful to think of responses to the environment and purposeful behaviour as potentially providing the starting points for the two main types of communication: communication for its own sake, and communication to achieve a goal.

Thinking of the sequence as being like that shown in Table 2.2 helps to make this distinction.

Table 2.2 Sequence of behaviours leading to communication

1. Voluntary behaviour: e.g. arm movements, leg movements, apparently random vocalisations which do not seem to be connected to environmental events in any way	
2(a) Responses to the environment: e.g. looks up when someone passes nearby, or when the door squeaks. Vocalises when another child vocalises, or in response to a particular member of staff speaking to another person. Smiles and looks when the wind waves the leaves of a tree just outside the window.	2(b) Purposeful behaviour: e.g. playing with a toy, walking deliberately towards something, picking up a piece of equipment.
3. Intentional communication: the child acts deliberately and spontaneously to attract someone else's attention: e.g. a child may reach out and touch you, look at you and smile or may initiate eye contact. They may vocalise when you have just left them to deal with someone else.	

Of course, even when we include responses to the environment, this sequence doesn't cover all behaviours – since not all behaviours can appropriately be interpreted as having communicative significance. There are other voluntary behaviours such as eating and drinking, stereotypies, and also involuntary behaviours such as coughs and sneezes. As we will see in the next chapter, although these behaviours may not be directly concerned with communication they are important because they may provide either the occasion for communication or a barrier to it. In particular, involuntary behaviours are important because they attract a high rate of adult responses.

Additionally, whereas some voluntary behaviours can be usefully interpreted as communication, especially when they change following a significant event, others may simply be indulged in for their own sake. A specific example should help to make this distinction clear. Susannah, one of the pupils who took part in the Contingency-Sensitive Environments Project, frequently moved her head as if looking around her. This behaviour, although voluntary, didn't normally seem to have any communicative significance. Sometimes, however, when a familiar adult came close to her, or when she heard another child vocalising, Susannah's head-moving increased and she might also smile and vocalise; this could appropriately be treated as an attempt to communicate, for example when Susannah responded to another child's vocalising by vocalising herself, an adult might say, 'Yes, Susannah. Isn't she noisy!'

One way, then, in which we can make sense of the behaviour of a person with PMLD is to interpret it in relation to events that are happening in the environment. This is, in fact, very similar to what adults do spontaneously with young infants without disabilities; who learn how to communicate without the adult being particularly aware of the part their own behaviour is playing in the process. However, when someone has PMLD, for all the reasons I've already mentioned, special efforts may be required to help them develop intentional communication.

The staff who took part in the Contingency-Sensitive Environments Project found being able to think about individual children's behaviour in terms of the sequence given in Table 2.2 helped them in their attempts to use the potential meaning of behaviour to develop communication. In fact, in the Contingency-Sensitive Environments Project we systematically examined the behaviours of each of the pupils in the classes involved in terms of the sequence given in Table 2.2. Discussion of each individual pupil used the form shown in Table 2.3 and focused around trying to place their various different behaviours within the sequence. The aim of this discussion (which took between ten minutes and half an hour for each pupil) was to give us an idea of both whereabouts in the sequence the majority of their behaviour fell, and what was currently their most sophisticated level of communication in the environment where we knew them.

The examples that follow show that, although it isn't always easy to sort out which behaviours an individual produces spontaneously, and which are responses to adult initiations, sharing views about the degree of communicative intent behind an individual's different behaviours can give everyone a deeper insight into the meaning these behaviours may have, and the type of environment that can help the individual to develop further.

> If you are coordinating a group working through the book together you will need to set aside some time (perhaps two half hours) to look at these examples and then hold a discussion about one of the pupils with whom you work.

Table 2.3 Record form for individual pupil

Child:			Date: 00/00/00
	Behaviour	Context	Frequency
INTENTIONAL COMMUNICATION			
PURPOSEFUL BEHAVIOUR			
RESPONSES TO THE ENVIRONMENT			
VOLUNTARY BEHAVIOUR			

Carol – A discussion about communicative intent

Carol was the first pupil we discussed during the Contingency-Sensitive Environments Project, and the discussion about her is given in more detail here than are the subsequent examples, in order to demonstrate the process by which staff who work with an individual can build on each other's knowledge to both obtain a profile of the individual's communicative abilities and the environments that facilitate their use and develop their own expertise in making sense of the behaviour of people with PMLD.

It became clear while we were talking about her, that people found it very difficult to identify behaviours that Carol engaged in spontaneously rather than as a response to another person. There seemed to be three reasons for this problem.

- First, most of her behaviours were in fact responses.
- Second, it was sometimes hard to decide whether a particular behaviour was spontaneous or a response to another person or to an event.
- Third, the staff who worked with Carol were accustomed to take the lead in interactions with her, and to looking for her responses to their actions, rather than to looking at what she was doing and following her lead.

This problem is not unique to Carol, nor to the group of staff who worked with her, but is one that occurs frequently in environments for people with PMLD, especially when education or training is involved (see for example the work by Houghton *et al.* mentioned in Chapter 1). Those of us who are teachers, in particular, often see our role as instructing our pupils, and this tendency is exacerbated by the public view that pupils go to school to gain knowledge and skills. When this tendency is combined with the low level of spontaneous behaviour shown by many pupils with PMLD it is easy for a vicious circle to develop in which the child learns that only responses are expected from them.

Thus, when we first started discussing Carol, someone suggested that her most sophisticated behaviour was sometimes smiling and making eye contact when an adult spoke to her. Of course, this was very clearly a response rather than a spontaneous behaviour, but knowing about it gave us an indication of the sort of spontaneous behaviours we might expect from Carol. Everyone was agreed that Carol only smiled in response to adult attention of some sort and never to attract attention or 'start a conversation'. Everyone was also agreed that Carol only sometimes smiled in response to an adult speaking to her. During the discussion it transpired that this was true not just of Carol's smiling, but of her other behaviours too; in fact several people thought of Carol as 'moody' for this reason.

As the smiling behaviour was a response we didn't try to discover whether there were consistent differences between the occasions when Carol smiled and those when she didn't, but if it had been a spontaneous behaviour, it would very probably have been useful to use some observations to find out. For instance, Carol may have smiled when some individuals spoke to her and not others, or she might only have smiled when the person speaking was standing very close and directly in her line of vision.

Establishing that Carol smiled only in response to someone speaking to her helped us to go on to find behaviours that she sometimes used spontaneously. Several people had noticed that Carol sometimes moved her head when things appeared in her line of vision – this was clearly a response to an environmental event; but there were two other things that she sometimes did that were possibly at a more sophisticated level than this. Carol occasionally vocalised; some people thought that she did this deliberately to attract attention, while others felt that she was probably responding to some environmental event such as hearing two familiar adults talking to each other, and still others wondered if it was simply a voluntary behaviour engaged in for its own sake.

Such disagreements between adults about whether a particular behaviour has communicative significance for an individual child are not unusual. For example, as was mentioned in Chapter 1, Wilcox *et al.* (1990) found that for some children with developmental disabilities there was sometimes only a minimal level of agreement between three adults who knew the child well (mother, teacher and speech and language therapist) about whether they were communicating or not. Additionally they found that adults interpreted very varying amounts of behaviour as communication when interacting with different children, and appeared to be using different definitions of 'communication'.

However, while these disagreements are not unusual (and may be even more common when someone has very severe disabilities), they may mean that certain individuals receive very inconsistent feedback about the effects of their behaviour. Pooling views about the meanings of an individual's behaviour can help to ensure that they receive consistent feedback, even when we are genuinely uncertain as to whether or not a particular behaviour has a particular meaning, and this can facilitate the development of communication.

To return to our discussion about Carol; in addition to agreeing that she smiled or vocalised in some circumstances, several people had noticed that Carol sometimes lifted her arm when a familiar adult was talking to a nearby child; although people couldn't agree about whether this behaviour was intentionally communicative (i.e. that Carol was deliberately trying to attract the attention of the adult), everyone was agreed that it was specific to the nearby presence of someone she knew working with another child. It seemed, then, that this arm-lifting behaviour was the most promising with regard to developing Carol's communication skills.

An important point about this behaviour is that it is not one that we would automatically and easily identify as being communicative – it isn't very readable. Additionally since it was both slow and silent, it could easily be missed by a busy adult who wasn't specifically looking out for it. So, although this arm-lifting seemed likely to be Carol's most sophisticated communicative behaviour (it was the only one everyone could agree only occurred in very specific circumstances), in terms of getting the sort of adult feedback that would help Carol to develop her communication skills the odds were stacked against her. However, once this arm-lifting behaviour had been identified as possibly intentionally communicative, people working near Carol could be on the lookout for it, ready to respond in an appropriate way. Additionally the chances of Carol getting a response to this behaviour could be increased by reviewing the way the classroom was organised (see Chapter 8).

As well as trying to ensure that everyone involved with Carol responded consistently to her arm-lifting, it would possibly have been useful to keep a record of the occasions when Carol vocalised. Vocal behaviour is the one that we most easily associate with communication, and is more easily noticed than many other behaviours. Additionally, research on caregiver-infant interaction shows that as the infant develops caregivers naturally begin to respond selectively to vocalisations (especially those accompanied by eye contact). This means that when a person does vocalise, for example in response to environmental events, this may well be the most appropriate behaviour to select for work on developing communication skills, because staff are likely to find it easier to respond to. Conversely, where a non-vocal behaviour (such as Carol's arm-lifting) is selected, we may have to make a particular effort to ensure that we respond to it consistently as communicative. In Carol's case, although she sometimes vocalised, people were unable to agree how sophisticated this vocalising was in terms of its communicative intent. Keeping a record could have highlighted any consistencies in Carol's vocalising and thus whether consistent responding to these vocalisations would provide an additional way of helping Carol to learn about communication. (See discussion about Jonathan in Chapter 6.)

Sanjeev – a discussion about voluntary behaviour

Sanjeev was a pupil with extremely complex needs and disabilities, including severe and poorly controlled epilepsy; and there was initially little agreement about the meaning of his behaviour. Some people suggested that Sanjeev responded to environmental events, whereas others were very sceptical about this, believing that these behaviours were involuntary – for example, Sanjeev would flinch if someone knocked his wheelchair or passed very close by. There was also disagreement about whether some of the other behaviours in Sanjeev's extremely limited repertoire were voluntary or not. For example, he sometimes seemed to smile; some people believed that these smiles represented minor epileptic seizures, while others felt that they were 'genuine'. However, people were eventually able to agree that some of Sanjeev's mouth and head movements were probably voluntary, and possibly changed in rate according to what was going on around him. Although they were at the least sophisticated level of communicative intent, these voluntary movements potentially provided an opening for the development of more sophisticated communication skills. For example, some people interpreted Sanjeev's head movements when sitting in his wheelchair as indicating discomfort; awareness that this might be the most likely explanation could lead to an agreement that when this behaviour was observed, staff would comment on Sanjeev's discomfort and offer to provide support so he could have his head up. This in turn might lead to the development of a 'conversation' where the adult also commented on the fact that Sanjeev was now more comfortable/could see better now etc. Additionally, responding to this behaviour in this consistent way would enable the hypothesis that Sanjeev's head movements indicated discomfort to be tested.

Sanjeev's mouth movements, which some people thought became more rapid when the classroom was busier, could be commented on as if that were true or as if they were in anticipation of some event. Thus even though, for Sanjeev, only very restricted voluntary behaviours could be identified, discussing these and their potential meaning offered the opportunity to provide an environment that would facilitate further development. Videoing Sanjeev in a variety of structured situations might also have helped with assessing the significance of his behaviours (see below).

However, as Sanjeev's voluntary movements were very limited indeed, some staff felt that it would also be appropriate to try and develop his contingency-awareness (his awareness of his ability to affect his environment) through exploring the use of switches and microtechnology. Such methods have been found to be effective with people with very severe learning and physical disabilities by a number of researchers. (See for example the review by Glenn and O'Brien 1994; and the more recent book by Bozic and Murdoch 1996; and Chapter 7.)

Jonathan – responding to environmental events

Jonathan's voluntary behaviours, like Sanjeev's, consisted mainly of mouth and head movements; however, he also occasionally vocalised. Discussion of Jonathan's behaviours highlighted the usefulness of supplementing such discussions with video and careful observation. Initially, almost everyone was unsure whether Jonathan's behaviours were purely voluntary or whether they occurred in response to environmental events. Examination of the video taken for the purposes of the project showed that Jonathan turned his head when an adult came to work near him, but out of his visual field. Additionally, the project team, with their privileged position as observers, had noticed that Jonathan's vocalisations were likely to occur when either another pupil vocalised or one particular member of staff spoke. Identifying these behaviours as responses to specific environmental events enabled staff to respond to them as if they were intentional communications; for example Flo, the member of staff to whose voice Jonathan vocalised, could make a variety of comments which treated Jonathan's behaviour as if it were an attempt to start up a conversation.

In all these examples discussion of the child's behaviours led to the identification of at least one voluntary behaviour which recurred with some degree of consistency in similar circumstances, and to which it was possible to attribute communicative significance. Except in the case of Carol's arm-lifting, there is no suggestion that the child intended to convey the meaning we gave the behaviour, rather that by responding as if the child had intended a meaning that is consistent with the environmental events that probably cause it (or at least co-occur with it) we can help them to learn to intend. By repeatedly having his increased head-turning interpreted as a request to be able to 'watch', and receiving an appropriate response, Jonathan may learn that he is able to produce responses from other people, and come to act deliberately in order to produce those responses. Clearly one aspect of an environment that facilitates the development of intentional communication is the child's actions receiving consistent, interpretive responses.

If you are coordinating a group, you should pause here and begin your discussions about the people with whom you work. For the first time it's a good idea to choose someone who you're not sure really communicates intentionally, but whom everybody knows quite well – this will give everyone the chance to participate in the discussion. Use the form in Table 2.3 to help focus your discussions.

First give everyone the chance to say what they think is the most sophisticated behaviour the child in question shows. For each behaviour mentioned you need to find out:

- the situation(s) in which it occurs;
- how often people think it occurs;
- *whether it is a spontaneous behaviour or a response.*

When the group have identified one or more potentially communicative behaviours for the individual you've chosen to consider, think about ways in which you can alter the environment to facilitate the development of more sophisticated communication from these behaviours.

Before going on to consider other individuals in the same way, it may be a good idea to read the section below on other ways of making sense of behaviour.

Other ways of making sense of behaviour

The link between some of the behaviours described in the previous section and the environmental events to which they may be a response is very easy to miss in a busy classroom or a crowded shopping centre, for example, and you may not even be convinced that this link exists (as in the case of Sanjeev increasing his rate of mouth movement when the level of activity in the classroom increases). In circumstances such as these it can be useful to carry out more structured observations of a particular individual's behaviour.

Such observations can either be based on an appropriate published assessment (see below) or on a home-made observation schedule. In either case it may be useful to video the assessment (see below). In Jonathan's case, for example, knowing that he sometimes vocalised, but not being sure if it was connected to a specific environmental event, you could use observation to check whether Jonathan, like many children, was vocalising in response to another person's voice. You might, for example, test whether Jonathan was responding to an adult's voice by setting up situations in which different members of staff were engaged in conversation and note any change in Jonathan's behaviour (see Table 2.4).

If, on the other hand, you wanted to establish whether Jonathan was vocalising when another child vocalised, you would need to use a recording system which captures the events happening around the time Jonathan vocalises (see Table 2.5). The type of observation shown in Table 2.5 could, in fact, equally well be used to record whether Jonathan's vocalisations were related to adults speaking. An additional advantage of using structured observation to supplement the information you already have about a child's potentially communicative behaviours is that we can obtain a rough picture of the frequency of the behaviour you are interested in, which can be useful when you are deciding where to concentrate your efforts (see next chapter).

Table 2.4 Record of Jonathan's reactions (if any) to adult speech

Member(s) of staff involved in conversation	Type of speech e.g. normal conversation with another adult, speaking to another child, raised voices	Jonathan's reaction (if any)
(Extend columns as needed.)		

Most published communication assessments do not provide sufficient detail at the pre-intentional level of communication to be useful in developing communication skills at this early level. However, since the first edition of this book was published, Coupe O'Kane and Goldbart (1998) have written a very useful and comprehensive book, which extends Goldbart's earlier work (Goldbart 1994) and includes two detailed assessments of early communication: the Affective Communication Assessment (ACA) and the Early Communication Assessment (ECA). The ACA can provide useful information to supplement that which can be gleaned from a discussion among people who know the individual well. The ACA consists of two sheets. The first is completed by presenting the child with a number of stimuli likely to elicit strong reactions; clusters of reactions can then be identified indicating things such as 'like' or 'reject'.

The second sheet is then completed to test out whether these reactions are general. Like the behaviours identified through discussion, information obtained through the ACA can provide the opportunity for the child to learn that his or her behaviour can produce responses from other people. The ECA provides a way of assessing people who are developing beyond the level of affective communication. For example, in earlier stages it enables staff to identify pupils' strategies for starting, maintaining and restarting interactions.

Table 2.5 Record of vocalisations made by Jonathan

Children vocalising immediately previously	Types of vocalisation e.g. happy babbling, crying loud, prolonged	Observed by

Damien – using video

Since the publication of the first edition of this book, I have worked with a number of groups of teachers who have recently begun teaching pupils with PMLD. During the course I have used video of individual pupils to help teachers develop their observation skills and learn to identify pupils' strengths (what they are able to do, the things they respond to, things they like, the sort of responses they make in different situations) and needs (what they need to learn next). Although the strengths-needs assessment is broadly based and is not just concerned with communication, I have found that groups often identify specific communicative behaviours such as anticipating another turn with a routine or filling in a turn in a song.

Most recently, I have worked with a pupil with very profound learning difficulties and his teacher. Using a strengths-needs assessment, Damien's teacher found it very difficult to identify any connections between his very limited range of behaviours and events in the environment. As with Sanjeev, it wasn't clear initially whether Damien had any voluntary behaviours at all. We videoed both me and Damien's teacher working with him because I wanted other people who couldn't be physically present to see what Damien was able to do and help with the assessment.

However, watching the video, we found that we were able to identify several behaviours that Damien seemed to use consistently to indicate particular meanings (mainly reject and dislike). His family also watched the video and quite independently confirmed our interpretations of these behaviours.

Videoing either a published assessment being carried out or during everyday activities and watching the video as a staff group can have a number of advantages:

- Most obviously, it can help staff explain exactly what behaviour they are describing.
- Where some staff interact only occasionally with particular individuals, it can help them become familiar with behaviours and their meaning and staff who cannot all be together during the time spent with pupils/clients can watch the same piece of video.
- In a quiet environment where no one is having to pay attention to other pupils/clients at the same time, behaviours can be spotted that would otherwise be missed.
- Because the same sequence of events can be watched a number of times, it may be possible to identify links between environmental events and the individual's behaviour.
- Video can facilitate discussion about the meaning of particular behaviours and can increase confidence about the way you are interpreting those behaviours.

This may be a good point at which to mention the challenging behaviour that some people with severe and profound learning difficulties show. There is good evidence that for at least some people challenging behaviours develop as a result of less extreme communications not being understood, and that understanding the meaning these behaviours convey can help us to alter the environment in a way that enables them to convey the same meanings in less distressing ways. There are now a number of publications that can be helpful in examining challenging behaviour with its possible communicative significance in mind (e.g. Durand 1990; Harris, Cook and Upton 1996).

> If you are coordinating a group, you need to arrange times when you can discuss each of the people with whom you work in order to identify their potentially communicative behaviours and how the development of these behaviours can be facilitated. This probably seems a massive task – after all, you may be working with five, six or even more people all of whom have

their own idiosyncratic ways of conveying meaning. However, you will find that you can usefully continue such discussions as you read the next chapter, which deals in more detail with deciding which behaviours to concentrate on, and organising the classroom to provide a responsive environment.

If you think that using video would help your discussions about some of the people with whom you work, you will need to consider both setting up the situations in which video is to be collected, and a structure for discussion. For example, you may want to video all or part of a structured assessment, and you may want to ask people watching the video to look initially for specific things (such as whether they can assign meanings to particular behaviours in specific circumstances). You may find it helpful to ask people to write these down initially so that subsequent discussions can focus on both the areas of agreement and the areas of disagreement.

In summary:

- We are likely to have problems in interpreting the behaviour of people with PMLD, but being aware of the potential difficulties such as delayed and idiosyncratic responses can help us to be sensitive to the meaning of their behaviour. *But* those who know an individual with PMLD well are often skilled in interpreting these behaviours.
- Thinking about the way in which communication develops in non-disabled infants (from involuntary reactions and simple voluntary behaviour through reactions to environmental events and purposeful behaviour to intentional communication) in relation to a particular individual can help us see the communicative potential in a wide variety of behaviours that are not yet intentional.
- Quite simple changes in the environment we provide can increase the chance of intentional communication developing from these pre-communicative behaviours.
- Useful supplementary information about the meaning of behaviour can be gained by using structured observation and published assessments designed for the purpose, and also through the use of video.

CHAPTER 3

Responding to People's Behaviour

In Chapter 1 I described a responsive environment as being composed of three parts:

- getting responses to your actions
- getting the opportunity to respond to the actions of others

and

- having the opportunity to take the lead in interaction.

This chapter deals in more detail with the first of these three aspects – getting responses to what you do.

I also mentioned in Chapter 1 that, in my initial investigations in classrooms for pupils with PMLD, I found that the pupils had very few opportunities for interaction of any sort. In that research I also found that even those interactions that did take place were dominated by the adult, and that children received responses to only a very small proportion of their spontaneous behaviours. We found a similar situation at the start of the Contingency-Sensitive Environments Project with the children receiving responses to only about one in ten of all their behaviours. Once again, staff dominated the interaction, taking the lead for about 90 per cent of the time. The issue of who takes the lead in interactions is dealt with in detail in Chapter 5 but it is also relevant in the context of responding to children's behaviours since an adult who is leading the interaction for a large percentage of the time is unlikely to be responding to the child's spontaneous behaviour even within the interaction. Of course, since there were always more children than adults in the classroom, many of the occasions when children didn't receive responses to their spontaneous behaviours were times when no one was working specifically with them. Levels of responses to behaviour that could easily be seen as communicative (such as vocalisations) were much higher. However, as I've already discussed (see Chapter 2), even staff who know an individual with PMLD very well may find it very hard to agree about when their behaviour should be regarded as communicative. Other researchers have reported very similar findings in adult environments (e.g. Hile and Walbran 1991; Kuder and Bryen 1993).

Responding to children's initiations

Spontaneous behaviour, and responses to it, can occur either when the individual is initially alone, and their behaviour attracts the attention of someone else, who responds in some way, or in the context of an interaction that is already taking place.

In the Contingency-Sensitive Environments Project, we found that even when pupils were working 1:1 with an individual member of staff, some pupils received many more responses to their behaviours than others. In fact, a complex picture emerged in which the extent to which staff responded to children's behaviours varied not only between individual children but according to the activity taking place, and the particular adult involved in the interaction. This is just the sort of picture that would be predicted from the work of Wilcox *et al.* (1990) reported in Chapter 1. In their investigation into the extent to which different adults interpreted the behaviour of non-verbal developmentally delayed toddlers as communication, they found huge variations between individuals. As noted in Chapter 1, one problem of this variability is that it means that some people are likely to receive very inconsistent responses to their communication attempts.

How many responses are enough?

The research on interactions between caregivers and infants which was discussed in Chapter 1 seems to imply that increased responding by caregivers to infants is always a good thing – regardless of the original level of responding. However, this needs to be seen in the light of repeated findings that infants with difficulties both do less, and receive fewer responses than those without difficulties. Indeed, some of these studies talk about the 'normalising' effect of their intervention on caregiver-infant interaction.

This raises some crucial questions. How many responses are enough? Or to put it another way, what proportion of behaviours need to receive responses in order to produce enhanced social and communication development? Is it desirable for a person with PMLD to receive responses to 100 per cent of their behaviours, and even if it is desirable, is there some good enough level of responding which it is more feasible for staff to aim at? Perhaps it is more important for people with PMLD to receive consistent responses to particular behaviours than for them to receive responses to absolutely all that they do. Certainly, much of the research with infants and their caregivers suggests that it is consistent, contingent and appropriate responding that is crucial. If 100 per cent responding is not desirable, what level is? Are different levels of responding desirable to behaviours that the individual produces when alone and those that s/he produces within an ongoing interaction?

The most fundamental of these questions is whether it is desirable for a person with PMLD to receive responses to 100 per cent of their behaviours either during an interaction and/or when they are initially alone. There is little research evidence specifically on this issue.

Responding during ongoing interactions

However, with regard to responses during the course of an interaction, some insight can be derived from examining work on interactions between caregivers and infants without difficulties, even though this has dealt almost exclusively with situations where the caregiver is asked to engage the infant in interaction, and results are usually given in terms of the proportion of the caregiver's behaviours that were responses to the infant (see Chapter 5) rather than the proportion of infant behaviours that received responses. Exceptionally, Kaye and Charney (1981) do give figures for the extent to which mothers respond to different types of behaviour from their two-year-old infants during three play situations (with a tea-set, a picture book and a Fisher-Price play family). They found that mothers respond to over 80 per cent of all their child's behaviours (90 per cent of the time to those that seem to demand a response and 77 per cent of the time to all other behaviours). Although these infants were operating at a more advanced developmental level than most people with PMLD, Kaye and Charney suggest that this picture mirrors that of earlier interactions. They argue that the adult takes the responsibility for keeping the interaction going even as the infant becomes more competent, and that progress occurs as the child gradually learns to take an equal share of responsibility for maintaining the interaction in successively more complex situations.

Second, theorists from a wide variety of perspectives see parental behaviour that is contingent on the infant's own behaviour as important for personality development. This view is supported by Breiner and Forehand (1982) who found evidence that young children who were developmentally delayed are more likely to receive undifferentiated positive responses to a wide variety of behaviours than children without difficulties. Similar results have also been found in relation to young children with Down's syndrome (e.g. Wishart 1991) and it has been suggested that this lack of clearly differentiated feedback may have a negative effect on development of social interaction skills.

Additionally it may be helpful to ask what normally happens in everyday human relationships, the sort of relationships that we regard as fulfilling for ourselves and desirable for the people we work with. In everyday relationships we do not receive responses to every single action, and whether or not we receive a response depends on the meaning of our actions as perceived by the other person or people who are able to observe them. Consequently, identical actions may receive very different responses on different occasions. For example, if, during a coffee evening, a friend observes me fidgeting, they might respond either by offering me a more comfortable seat (on the assumption that I am uncomfortable), or by trying to bring the evening to a close (on the assumption that I am bored), or they may not respond at all (because they see me as someone who often fidgets for no particular reason). In any of these instances their interpretation of my behaviour and their response to it may or may not be appropriate. There are, of course, many occasions when as adults we do not respond to each other's behaviour, because we do not regard it as requiring a response. This again highlights our predisposition to respond to the behaviour of others in terms of its meaning (how we interpret it) rather than its form (what the person is actually doing).

So then, for the great majority of people with PMLD, an appropriate interactive environment is likely to be one where their behaviours are responded to discriminatively, with those behaviours that have most communicative potential receiving high levels of response, while behaviours that appear to be involuntary or engaged in purely for their own sake will receive much lower levels. However, like the environment experienced by a young infant, what is appropriate will change as the person changes, and for those people at the very earliest levels of development, who currently do very little, it may be appropriate to respond to everything that they do, at least initially.

Responses to behaviours that occur when the individual is initially alone

Although there is no research on how caregivers respond to infants' behaviours outside the context of an ongoing interaction, investigators in other areas suggest that here too it is contingent responses that are important. For example, work on the development of contingency awareness using microtechnology demonstrates that it is important for the child to get feedback telling them that a particular action has caused a particular effect. Suggestions as to how research in this area can usefully be applied in environments for people with PMLD are given in Chapter 7.

How do different situations affect the responses of staff to people with PMLD?

In my research I have found that staff in PMLD classes generally respond to between a quarter and a third of children's behaviours when an interaction is already taking place, a considerably lower proportion than that found by Kaye and Charney; although as I have already said this proportion varied from time to time according to a number of factors.

If receiving responses to what you do is important for developing communication and interactive skills therefore, and pupils with PMLD generally receive a smaller proportion of responses than an infant functioning at a similar developmental level would from a caregiver, it may be helpful to compare situations where pupils with PMLD generally received high levels and those where they received low levels of response to their actions.

Types of behaviour that attract a response

In the Contingency-Sensitive Environments Project we initially found that, whereas actions that were clearly· or very probably intended to be communicative were responded to more often than other spontaneous behaviours, 'responses to the environment' were unlikely to receive responses from staff. ('Responses to the environment', as was explained in Chapter 2, are behaviours such as looking up when someone passes nearby, or when the door squeaks, or smiling and looking when the wind waves the leaves of a tree just outside the window. They also include responses to other people who are not actually interacting with the individual concerned; such as vocalising when another child/client vocalises, or in response to a particular member of staff speaking to another person.) The behaviours to which staff responded most frequently, however, were involuntary behaviours – sneezes and coughs. Whether the child was already being interacted with or not, these behaviours attracted responses almost 100 per cent of the time. There are probably three reasons why this was so: first, coughs may be distressing and painful, and occasionally even life-threatening; second, in British culture it is usual to respond to coughs and sneezes, particularly when a child is involved. Third, these behaviours are usually very noticeable, involving loud noises and sometimes quite violent body movements. Although these involuntary behaviours have no communicative significance, the high level of response to them is positive in that it demonstrates that even in busy environments staff are able to respond contingently and consistently to particular behaviours.

In my previous research (where I classified children's behaviours not according to their level of communicative sophistication, but according to type) I found that vocal behaviours were significantly more likely to receive responses than non-vocal behaviours. Other researchers have also found that adults are more likely to respond to vocal than non-vocal behaviours. Taken together, these findings highlight the fact that the more you communicate (or the more like communication your behaviour appears), the more likely others are to communicate with you. This further underlines the importance of being sensitive to the meaning of behaviours that would not normally be interpreted as communicative, and that may not be particularly prominent in a busy environment.

Personal factors

In the Contingency-Sensitive Environments Project we found clear differences between the children who received the lowest number of responses and other members of the class. They tended to have fewer physical and more behavioural problems and to be unpopular with staff. The children who received the highest levels of response were a very mixed group, including those from each school with the most profound learning difficulties and three physically attractive young children who were already communicating intentionally. In that to some extent these results mirror those of other researchers in a variety of environments for people with PMLD and SLDs, these findings were not particularly unexpected. However, they highlight the need for strategies to ensure that those people least likely to receive responses to their actions do in fact do so.

Activities

Children were also more likely to receive responses to their actions during some activities than others. Children's initiations during drinks received a higher than average level of response in both schools, as they did during physiotherapy in School 1. However, during language and individual work sessions (in School 2) children received a considerably lower than average level of responses to their initiations.

Although superficially these results may seem surprising, drinks sessions in both schools and physiotherapy sessions in School 1 did have a number of factors in common. First, they involved a staff member working individually with one pupil at a time, and in close physical proximity to them – thus they were in a good position to observe any spontaneous behaviour engaged in by the pupil. Second, these activities involved repeated series of actions – the pupil is given a sip of drink, they swallow, they open their mouth and are given another sip of drink. Within this context, one behaviour – the pupil opening their mouth – is clearly understood by the member of staff as an initiation on the part of the pupil – they want or are ready for 'more'. Finally, these activities were repeated on a regular daily basis, providing a framework that was familiar to both staff member and pupil, and within which pupil initiations were expected.

By contrast, in activities in which pupils received a low level of response to their actions, the staff member was often looking for specific responses from the pupil to her initiations. In language, for example, the staff member might be engaged in activities that were designed to elicit vocalisation from a particular pupil. Additionally, these activities took place on a regular basis and it might be that the pupils had learned that within these contexts they were not expected to initiate interactions. In other activities in which pupils received a lower than average level of response to their actions, the adult might well be positioned to the pupil's rear or side, making it difficult for them to observe the pupil. For example, some physiotherapy sessions in School 2 involved the adult sitting with the pupil in their lap facing away from them.

Strategies for increasing your own responses

> If you are coordinating a group working through this book together, you may want to read the whole of the section on strategies and decide which are most likely to be appropriate in your particular situation.

Perhaps the simplest strategy for increasing your own responses is to make sure that you are positioned so that you can monitor the behaviour of the person or people you are working with. Most of the time this will involve making sure that you can see them. In many of the illustrations in this chapter and in Chapter 4, staff have positioned themselves strategically so they can monitor the behaviour of one or more pupils (e.g. Ann in Figure 3.1 and Penny in Figure 4.6). Sometimes, however, being able to monitor an individual's behaviour may involve ensuring that you can hear by reducing the level of extraneous noise, or being in physical contact so that you can feel a reaction such as stilling or maintaining contact. For example, when I was asked to assess Seán recently, his father told me that Seán would 'ask' for a game of 'ride a cock-horse' to be continued by jigging up and down slightly. This was a very important observation because it turned out to be the most sophisticated communication behaviour that Seán had. Gently holding the hand of the person positioned next to you while working with a group may enable you to notice them beginning to get restless, and to treat this positively as a request for a break from the group.

If you are in the habit of working with someone from behind, perhaps in order to support them, you could discuss with the physiotherapist or other colleagues whether an alternative working position is possible.

Staff who took part in the Contingency-Sensitive Environments Project also found two other simple strategies helpful in responding more to children's behaviours:

- becoming aware of which pupils were receiving the lowest levels of response, and
- being aware of the potential for communication of behaviours that had previously seemed meaningless.

Ways in which you can become aware of the potential meaning of behaviours that are otherwise difficult to interpret have been discussed in Chapter 2. Here I look at how you can become aware of which pupils/clients are receiving the lowest level of response and then go on to look at some other practical strategies for increasing your responses to what the pupil or client is doing, both when you are working specifically with them and when they are initially alone.

During the Contingency-Sensitive Environments Project, feedback provided to staff included graphs demonstrating the amount and type of interaction being experienced by individual pupils. This feedback, combined with a greater awareness of the potential meaning of individuals' behaviours, enabled staff to respond more to those children who initially experienced particularly low levels of adult response to their actions. Thus, while at the beginning of the project some children received nine times as many responses as others; during the course of the intervention this difference decreased to six times. In addition staff became more discriminating in their responses, responding more frequently to children's communication.

The type of feedback provided by the project staff was derived from detailed observations. Such observations are rarely practical except in a research context. However, there are a number of ways of making yourself more aware of the extent to which you respond to what different individuals do. The following exercise need take only a few minutes, and can provide you with feedback about your own behaviour, which, while it will not be as accurate as that obtained from detailed observations, can provide the basis for action.

Strategies that are particularly useful when the individual is initially alone

Exercise
Select two of the individuals from among those with whom you work regularly, preferably one with whom you find it easy to get on and one whom you find it more difficult to work with.

At the end of a period when you have been at least partly responsible for both individuals concerned, try to write down how many times you responded to something they did.

- What did the person do?
- Was it an entirely spontaneous behaviour or did it follow something you did?
- How did you respond?

Compare your responses to the two individuals. Discount, for the purpose of this exercise, any occasions when they were responding to a request from you, and you simply praised their compliance.

If you are coordinating a group, you may want to structure this exercise ensuring that everyone has the opportunity to carry it out, and by making time for them to write down their observations immediately after the period when they have been monitoring their own behaviour.

Figure 3.1a Although she is working with Sonya, Ann positions herself so she can see Leanne and Emma

Figure 3.1b She is in a good position to respond to Leanne, when she turns towards her

Responding to people you are not currently working with

Simply carrying out this exercise is likely to mean that you respond more to the individuals concerned, because it will sensitise you to the possibility that you have been missing opportunities to respond. But you may also be aware of a conflict between continuing with what you are doing with one individual and responding to another individual with whom you are not currently working. This problem is likely to become even clearer if you have the opportunity to take a video of an individual over a period of time when they are not being worked with individually. You do not necessarily need someone to be behind the lens of the video camera to obtain useful material for this purpose. If you can find an appropriate suspension point, you can simply hang the camera in a position where it can 'see' most of the room, including the person you are interested in. In this case, a view that includes most of the room is likely to be more useful than a close-up of just one person since it is more likely to enable you to observe the relationship between the individual's behaviour and other things going on in the room. Remember you will need to structure your review of the video to enable you to make the appropriate connections (see Chapter 2). In this instance you might want to be particularly on the lookout for behaviours which suggest that an individual is protesting about being left at the end of an interaction, for example beginning to vocalise when the staff member moves from them to another individual, or behaviours that suggest that an individual is attracted by what is going on nearby.

In the Contingency-Sensitive Environments Project we took five minutes of video of each pupil about every two weeks. In one physiotherapy session the pupil we were filming, Elizabeth, had already received her physio for the day and was lying adjacent to a member of staff working with another pupil. On several occasions Elizabeth lifted her head and shoulders off the floor and looked and smiled towards the member of staff. This was unnoticed by the staff member who was concentrating on delivering physio and not facing towards her. Since this was a sophisticated initiation for Elizabeth, *and* was probably a deliberate attempt to start an interaction, when the staff saw the video they felt that they should take action to ensure that such initiations were responded to in the future.

One simple strategy for doing so would be to make sure that the member of staff closest to an individual not currently being worked with was facing in their direction (as well as attending to the person they were working with). For example, in Figure 3.1a, by positioning herself to the side of Sonia while she is working with her, Ann is in a good position to respond to Leanne when she turns towards her (Figure 3.1b) and had a clear idea of initiations to which it was particularly important to respond.

In Figure 3.2 Penny responds to Tracey although she is working with Darren. The photograph in Figure 3.3 shows a group game (see Chapter 6 for further details). Like Ann in the music group shown in Figures 3.1a–b, Penny has the children

Figure 3.2 Penny responds to Tracey although she is working with Darren

Figure 3.3 Playing a group game

sitting in a semi-circle so that they are encouraged to watch what others are doing and staff are able to see their responses. Here Darren is interested in what Penny and Ben are doing with a small ball that lights up and buzzes when warmed by a hand and Penny is positioned so that she is likely to notice his interest and respond.

To return to Elizabeth's attempt to attract attention by looking and smiling towards the member of staff working near her, staff concerned with this particular example felt it should be possible for them to respond appropriately to initiations of this type even while working with another individual, as a comment addressed to her such as 'Are you watching so-and-so's exercises?' would be sufficient acknowledgement. However, not all people with PMLD would know that they were being spoken to from a distance; or a greater level of response might be desirable. (For example, it might have been appropriate to offer to help Elizabeth sit up 'so she could see better'.) Other strategies for resolving the conflict may be required. (See also the example of Tanya in Chapter 5.)

It is also important to remember that people with PMLD may need to learn that particular communication strategies are not equally effective in all situations. Elizabeth's strategy of looking and smiling was ineffective partly because it was inappropriate to the situation where the person whose attention she was trying to attract had their back towards her. Barber and Goldbart (1998) cite a very similar example of a teenager, Hanna, who similarly initiated towards adults who were close by but not oriented towards her. Altering the organisation of the environment so that Elizabeth's (or Hanna's) initiations are more likely to be noticed by staff is only part of the answer. Barber and Goldbart further argue that simply teaching additional strategies may be ineffective (or simply confusing) if the individual concerned has not learned to recognise the critical features of situations in which their initiation attempts are successful. However, this may depend on how these new strategies are taught. For example, Elizabeth could be encouraged to vocalise in addition to lifting herself off the ground, perhaps through use of a switch that produces sounds likely to elicit vocalisations from her (see Chapter 7), or through the intervention of an additional staff member who encourages her to call out. However, as Barber and Goldbart suggest, people like Elizabeth and Hanna also need to learn to discriminate occasions on which adults are oriented to respond to the strategies they use. This might perhaps be achieved by providing some cue, such as exaggerated facial features, that the staff member's attention is available.

It is perhaps appropriate to add a word of caution about using video at this point. Easily used video cameras have revolutionised some aspects of observation and assessment, and as in the example of Damien given in Chapter 2, video can change the way we view a particular individual. However, to be useful, video needs to be collected in a carefully structured way and watched with a clear idea of the type of events you are looking for. Before starting to video you should be clear as to whether you are going to video a session that has been specifically organised for the purpose (for instance, a communication assessment) or whether you want a more general picture, for example of the interactions someone experiences. This will help you decide whether a close-up of the individual or a wider view will be most useful on this particular occasion. You also need to remember that the video is being used as a working tool, just like a record sheet or an IEP page. What's important is the information you can get from it, not whether it's technically a good picture.

> If you are coordinating a group, and intend to use video, you will need to remember that people can find watching video of themselves, or allowing others to watch it stressful; and it is worth laying down some simple ground rules for all those involved. For example, if a member of staff has been videoed working closely with an individual, as Mary and I were when we were trying to assess Damien, a good rule of thumb is that if someone didn't respond to a particular behaviour it was most probably because they were unable to see (or hear) it. Short extracts demonstrating exactly what you mean are a better use of time than watching the whole of a tape. Positive examples are much more effective than negative ones, and people involved should be clear that you will only be showing them engaged in the sort of interactions you are hoping to promote. You should also try and show examples of all members of staff interacting with clients in a positive way at different times. This means that to use video effectively you need to have the time available to watch each tape you collect and select appropriate examples from it. (Using video in this way is discussed in more detail in Chapter 8 in relation to positive monitoring.)

Organisational strategies

The strategy suggested above for ensuring that Elizabeth received responses to her initiations is essentially an organisational strategy. It involves setting priorities: deciding that if Elizabeth is deliberately trying to initiate an interaction with a staff member working near to her, ensuring that she gets a response is more important (at that particular time) than working uninterruptedly with someone else, and specifying who is going to be working close to her during the session in question. During periods of time when some people are not being specifically worked with, organisational strategies can help in:

- ensuring that people still get responses to what they do;
- equalising staff time between pupils/clients, so that those who are least likely to engage in deliberate communication do not miss out further.

Of course, in many organisations, for much of the time staff and clients or pupils will be involved in activities on an individual or small group basis. However, there are still some occasions when a group of staff is responsible for a larger group of clients or pupils, and research suggests that it is precisely in these sorts of circumstances that individuals are most likely to have their initiations ignored.

Research has also shown that when groups of staff are responsible for large groups of clients or pupils with PMLD, it is generally more effective (in terms of engagement in activities and the distribution of staff time among clients/pupils) for most staff members to have a particular role in relation to the whole pupil/client group than for them to have responsibility for a sub-group of clients/pupils. For example, at a particular time one staff member may be responsible for assisting anyone who needs to use the toilet, while other members of staff may have responsibilities such as ensuring that everyone is engaged in an activity of their choice etc. One form of organisation that provides clear roles for staff is 'Room Management' which has been extensively researched in environments for people with PMLD (see Ware 1994). Such systems are not primarily concerned with the interactive environment. However, in my previous research (Ware 1990) I found that staff in classes using the Room Management system were more likely to respond to children's behaviours, and more likely to respond positively than when other systems were in use. The use of Room Management also significantly reduced the extent to which more able pupils within the group received the lion's share of the available adult attention. Jones *et al.* (1999), in a study of small staffed houses for adults with severe to profound learning difficulties, similarly found that an organisational strategy that, like Room Management, was deliberately focused on increasing engagement was effective in equalising the distribution of staff time between clients.

Additionally a system such as 'Room Management' might be modified by assigning one member of staff to the role of 'responder' responsible for responding consistently to potentially communicative behaviours from clients/pupils who are not working individually with another member of staff in order to reduce the likelihood of individuals having their initiations ignored. Of course, it would also be possible to provide such a role within other forms of organisation.

Strategies that are particularly useful during ongoing interactions

Organisational strategies can be of great help in clarifying the responsibilities of staff for ensuring that each individual within a group situation receives appropriate responses to their actions, especially when they are not engaged in specific individual or group work. However, there are many occasions when, as an individual member of staff, you may be working with one individual pupil/client in a wide range of situations – anything in fact from a shopping trip to an individual skill teaching session. Additionally over the course of a day or a week, you may work individually with a comparatively large number of people. In the Contingency-Sensitive Environments Project, although staff successfully increased their responding to those pupils who were receiving fewest responses; even so, pupils received responses to less than 40 per cent of their spontaneous behaviours during ongoing interactions, compared with the more than 80 per cent of responses received by infants without difficulties from their mothers. Additional strategies are therefore required to ensure that individuals with PMLD receive high rates of responses.

A number of investigators have remarked that one surprising fact about interactions between mothers and their infants with disabilities is that, although the infant produces fewer obviously meaningful behaviours than an infant without disabilities, the mother responds to just as high a proportion of these behaviours as do the mothers of infants without disabilities. Kaye and Charney (1981) suggest that, in the absence of meaningful behaviours, the mother takes any behaviour that the infant produces and attributes meaning to it. The behaviour may be treated either as a response to something the mother has said or done or as a new initiation on the part of the infant. A similar technique can be adopted during ongoing interactions with an individual with PMLD. For example, if, during an art session, you have asked the individual with whom you are working to 'spread the blue paint' (with their fingers), and they do not respond, but a few seconds later they vocalise, you could respond to this either as a new topic of conversation – 'Oh you'd rather chat than paint would you? Fair enough' or as a response to your request, 'You think it needs some more paint first? Right, here you are.' Of course, it's important that such interpretations of behaviour are appropriate to the individual, for example that adults are addressed as adults.

Whether it is most appropriate to respond to all behaviours or selectively to those that are communicatively most sophisticated will depend on the individual's level of functioning. Looking at the behaviour of the people with whom you work in the way described in Chapter 2 provides a basis for deciding whether or not behaviours should be responded to selectively and, if so, which behaviours to respond to. However, where individuals have a range of behaviours at a particular level of communicative sophistication – whether, for example, this is simply a range of voluntary behaviours or a range of responses to the environment – some way of selecting those that provide the most useful focus for development is required. In this context, the following 'rules of thumb' are useful:

- Behaviours that can easily be developed into conventional communication – such as vocalisations which might develop into speech, or arm and hand movements which could develop into signs. (An additional reason for selecting vocalisations where possible is that research shows that they are more likely to attract responses.)
- Behaviours that are easy to observe – these behaviours are more likely to attract a high rate of response in busy situations.
- Behaviours that occur fairly regularly so there are plenty of opportunities for responding to them.

Even if you are working through this book as a member of a group who all work in the same situation, the prospect of trying to respond selectively to particular behaviours for each individual may seem overwhelming. A good strategy to adopt to ensure you don't become overwhelmed is to select one individual and try and respond consistently to one thing that they do. So if, for example, one of the people you work with regularly looks up when the door squeaks, you may (ideally after discussion with other relevant members of staff) decide to respond by telling her who has come into the room, and sometimes asking additionally if she wants to say 'hello'. It's important to try and select a behaviour that occurs fairly frequently and that is at an advanced level of communication for the particular individual. It's also important to find a way of responding that feels natural to you, since you are trying to make this way of responding part of your normal repertoire of behaviours, and to keep the interactions between yourself and the people you work with natural and enjoyable. For example Ann, an expert teacher I have been working with recently in Dublin, told us that she had deliberately refrained from oiling the squeaky door of her individual workroom, because it gave Sonya and Emma, who both have severe visual impairments, the opportunity to react and Ann herself to respond as if they were initiating a conversation with her. For example, when Catherine came into the room, Ann responded to Emma's reaction by saying 'Who's that? That's Catherine; she wants to know if you're having lunch today.'

If you are coordinating a group working through this book together, once you have discussed several of the people with PMLD with whom you work in the way described in Chapter 2, you might suggest that each member of staff selects one person, and one of their potentially communicative behaviours to respond to, as a first step. As I said in the first edition, people don't need to say which individual they've decided to concentrate on or all to respond in the same way; since each person needs to respond in a way with which they are personally comfortable, if this way of working is going to become part of their normal behaviour. However, the effectiveness of this strategy is likely to be enhanced if staff are able to agree on appropriate behaviours and responses to those behaviours. Ensuring that each pupil or client has been selected by at least one member of staff is also important since each member of staff will have their personal preferences among clients.

Another strategy, which has been found useful in producing increased levels of responding both in interactions between caregivers and infants with difficulties and between staff and young adults with PMLD, is simply to imitate the behaviour produced by the individual. Using this strategy can not only increase the level of responses the person gets to their behaviour, but also decrease the extent to which the more competent interactive partner dominates the interaction. The use of imitation will therefore be explained in detail in Chapter 5 which looks at enabling people with PMLD to take the lead in interaction.

What if a person doesn't seem to want to interact?

For some people with PMLD, the problem seems to be that they simply don't want to interact with others. They may do very little spontaneously, so that simply responding to what they do, still leaves them engaged in interaction for only a very small proportion of the day. They may also reject approaches from staff or other pupils/clients who try to engage them in interaction. For some people this unwillingness to engage in interaction may reflect previous experiences of an unresponsive environment, where they have learned that there is nothing they can do to influence what happens. In this situation microtechnology may help (see Chapter 7), but there are also simple interactive strategies that can be employed. For example, it may be possible to encourage the person to 'do more' by engaging in the type of games and routines that caregivers use with infants.

Ann is very skilled at encouraging her pupils to become more active both by using technology, and through games and routines. For example, in Figures 3.4a and 3.4b she plays a peek-a-boo game with Leanne. This increases Leanne's general activity level as she turns from side to side. With Sonia, Ann used favourite musical instruments and songs with which Sonia would join in. When playing games of this sort, it is important to be on the lookout for signs of over-stimulation, and to stop when the individual indicates they have had enough. With someone who is difficult to engage in interaction, it's very tempting to continue too long with an activity that appears to be 'working'. However, research with caregivers and their infants with disabilities suggests that continuing too long can be counterproductive (e.g. Field 1983).

Where an individual seems to reject interaction or to be absorbed in self-stimulatory behaviour, Intensive Interaction (Nind and Hewett 1994; Hewett and Nind 1998) may be useful as part of an overall strategy designed to encourage them to engage in social interaction.

Summary

In this chapter I have outlined a number of personal and organisational strategies that can be used to increase the extent to which people with PMLD get responses to their actions in group situations. Implementing organisational strategies needs the

Figure 3.4a and b Anne plays peek-a-boo with Leanne

cooperation of everyone who works in a particular situation, but personal strategies can be implemented by one individual in a wide range of situations, although they are likely to be more effective if they are adopted by a whole-staff team.

Organisational strategies

- Ensure that when an individual is not being specifically worked with, a member of staff who is working with someone else can see them, is aware of the ways in which they can respond and the behaviours that it is particularly important to respond to.
- Use a roles system where a member of staff has responsibility for responding to those who are not currently specifically engaged in individual or group work.
- Use a system that is likely to equalise staff time between pupils/clients.

Personal strategies

- Whenever you are working with an individual, ensure that you are positioned so that you can observe any initiations they make and avoid being distracted

by what other members of staff are doing or saying.
- Become aware of which people are receiving the lowest levels of response by monitoring your own behaviour.
- Become aware of the potential for communication of the behaviours in each individual's repertoire.
- Select behaviours to respond to on the basis of their communicative potential.
- Start small – select one individual and try and ensure you respond consistently to one thing that they do.
- Use games and routines with people who seem to do very little to increase their general level of activity and give yourself more to respond to.

CHAPTER 4

Starting a Conversation, Giving the Child a Chance to Reply

In the last two chapters we were concerned with developing ways of increasing our ability to interpret the behaviours of people with PMLD and with increasing the extent to which we respond appropriately to those behaviours as attempts at communication. This chapter is about your attempts to start a conversation with someone with PMLD and the opportunities they have within that conversation to respond to what you do – the second aspect of the interactive environment.

Why start a conversation?

Just as (as we saw in the last chapter) the context is important when we are responding to the behaviour of an individual with PMLD, so it is when we are initiating the interaction. In particular, our aim or purpose in starting the interaction plays a large part in shaping the way it proceeds.

There are a number of different reasons for attempting to initiate an interaction with another person. We may, for example, have a functional purpose in mind, getting assistance to move a heavy object, asking them to clear their things away, offering assistance with the washing up, helping them to get ready to go home, taking them to an activity in another room etc.

The 'conversation' may have a teaching purpose: for example, we may be demonstrating the way in which the lawnmower can be adjusted or we might be concerned with increasing an individual's skills and independence in preparing food and start an interaction with them focused on this task.

Alternatively, we may be starting a conversation purely for its own sake, as with any friend or colleague. In this case the topic of the conversation (whether it is yesterday evening's episode of *Neighbours* or the implications of a 'leaked' government decision to impose VAT on children's clothes) may be less important than the pleasure we derive from the interaction. This example also illustrates another important reason why we engage in interactions with others, and that is because we believe that interactions are capable of influencing those who participate in them.

Of course, an interaction often has more than one purpose. We may respond to a general appeal for help with the washing up both because we can see that there is a great deal to be done, *and* because we enjoy the company of the person requesting help. On one occasion the *outcome* of our discussion on motorway driving may be relatively unimportant compared with the pleasure of sparring with a close friend; on another we may be much more interested in convincing the other participant of our views than in the interaction itself.

Getting the child's attention

An interaction with someone with PMLD may have any of these purposes (although research suggests that the majority of interactions between a member of staff and a person with PMLD are of a functional nature; e.g. O'Connell 1994). Conversations in differing contexts have different characteristics, different possibilities for development and different pitfalls. However, particularly in relation to the actual start of the conversation, they also have things in common. Starting a conversation successfully involves checking in some way that the other person is ready and willing to participate, getting their attention, and signalling to them that it is a conversation we want and not a monologue. Most important of these is getting the other person's attention.

If we wish to start a conversation with a colleague who is working or reading on the other side of the room, we may go about this in one of several ways. For example, we may monitor their behaviour, waiting for them to pause in their work, look up from their reading etc. before speaking. Alternatively we may say their name and then wait for them to look up, or give some other indication that we have their attention before continuing. In another situation we may wait until we can make eye contact with the other person before speaking. This is a strategy that we might well employ when there are several participants in the conversation rather than just two, or in a situation such as a check-out queue or canteen.

It can be useful, then, to think of the business of getting the other person's attention in order to start a conversation as being divided into two stages, first checking that their attention is available and then attracting and holding it. Any conversation, though, involves at least two participants. If the reader replies 'uh, huh' and continues with their book, or the person sitting opposite in the canteen looks away as we catch their eye, particularly if this is repeated when we make a second or third attempt, we may conclude that they are not willing to participate in a conversation at that moment. Often we employ strategies such as these for signalling our desire to participate in a conversation, or our unwillingness to do so, without really being aware of it. People with PMLD are no different from anyone else in not always wanting to interact with us and if our attempts at interaction are going to be mutually satisfying we need to learn to read the ways in which they indicate that, just at the moment, they don't feel like being involved with us. I will return to this point in the next chapter.

Getting a word in edgeways – checking the availability of attention

The simple strategy of saying someone's name and then pausing is one we often use for getting the attention of someone when we need to interact with them for some functional purpose, such as asking them to get ready for a meal. If, for example, a child is absorbed in playing with their toys, or engrossed in watching television, we may call their name and pause before continuing, repeating this (perhaps with additional emphasis) if there is no response at first. Even this strategy, though, is more likely to be successful if we pick our moment for employing it with care, choosing a time when the other person does not have all their attention fully engaged elsewhere.

So picking the right moment to begin an interaction or, to be more accurate, picking an appropriate moment, is important in any interaction. But it is particularly important when the person with whom you wish to start your 'conversation' has PMLD. Human beings have only a limited capacity for attention, and in general terms that capacity increases with increasing (developmental) maturity, as does the ability to divide attention between two simultaneous events. Someone with PMLD, because they are developmentally very young, has both a much more limited capacity for attention and more difficulty in dividing their attention than an adult without difficulties. Secondly, impairments in the area of vision or hearing may make your efforts to attract their attention less obvious. Thirdly, because many people with PMLD have experienced a rather impoverished environment, they may have become very absorbed in self-stimulatory behaviours.

However, just as we often employ signals that show whether or not we are ready to participate in a conversation, without really being aware of the process involved; we may equally be unaware of some of the clues that tell us when we have a good chance of capturing another person's attention. Even if you are aware of these clues you may still have real difficulty in applying them to the people with PMLD with whom you work, because their signals may be less clear than those of people who are already skilled interactors.

The examples that follow of successful attempts to capture the attention of people with PMLD highlight the importance of careful observation in identifying times when attempts to begin an interaction are most likely to succeed, and the range of strategies that can be employed to make someone's attention available. You may also find these examples helpful in identifying the type of behaviours that may signal that an individual's attention is available to be 'caught'.

If you are a group coordinator, you will need to read through the examples before discussing them with the group. Be prepared to draw parallels between the examples given and particular individuals familiar to the group – this will both help the group see the relevance of the examples and facilitate the exercise given on page 56. For instance, you may have a client who, like Tanya, fusses when left or who sometimes seems to be listening to or watching events.

David – waiting for a pause in continuous behaviour

David is a five-year-old who can walk around, hold things, and coordinate his hands sufficiently to rub an object he is holding in one hand with the other. However, he rarely makes eye contact, and appears to take no notice of most attempts to attract his attention. He has severe epilepsy with both occasional major seizures and frequent brief absences. His rubbing of toys is often accompanied by more or less continuous vocalisations of an uh-uh-uh type. Because he appeared not to respond when spoken to or to many other classroom noises, his teacher was concerned that David might be deaf. Joe, the peripatetic teacher for children with hearing impairments, observed David for some time and then sounded the bell he used to test young children's hearing. David immediately turned to the sound, and this demonstration was repeated on several occasions. Joe was thus able to establish that David had at least some hearing. By observing David acutely he had been able to pick an appropriate moment to try and attract David's attention, in fact he waited until David momentarily stopped both his uh-uh noise and his rubbing of the toy he was holding.

The strategy Joe employed to gain David's attention parallels that of waiting for the reader to look up from their book before speaking to them. Essentially, the observer waits for a pause, however brief, in the ongoing stream of behaviour and seizes it to get their 'word' in. Of course, to do this successfully with David, Joe had first to observe David closely in order to discover if there were times when David was less self-absorbed, and then catch him in one of these moments.

Clive – catching an alert moment

Clive was a pupil from one of the research project classes who had very profound learning difficulties and physical disabilities. He often seemed unwell and his breathing could be very difficult. Much of the time he was at school he spent either asleep or in a state that seemed somewhere between sleep and waking, showing little consciousness of the things going on around him. Often when he was timetabled for a particular activity he would be asleep. On one morning, he had slept through a language session, despite the best efforts of the member of staff to wake him, and had continued to sleep as he was taken to another classroom for his mid-morning drink. As drinks began, and Clive's teacher, Penny, was starting to help two of the other pupils, Clive suddenly opened his eyes wide. Penny, seizing on the opportunity this offered, turned to him and began a brief interaction.

Tanya – alert and 'listening'

Tanya, another pupil in the same class, had a much wider range of behaviours than Clive and, although she had profound learning difficulties, was functioning on a more advanced developmental level. Tanya had good head control when she was in a supporting chair, and would lift her head so that she could see what was going on around her. She also had some arm and hand movements which were probably voluntary, and could grasp an object placed in her fingers. Staff described her as fussing if she didn't get their attention; she would often vocalise loudly when left, and sometimes when staff were interacting with other pupils nearby. In addition to 'fussing', Tanya had a posture which staff described as 'listening' in which she would sit quiet and alert with her head up. Staff correctly interpreted this posture as signalling that Tanya's attention was available to be 'caught' for an interaction.

On one occasion, for example, Penny noticed Tanya in her listening posture as she was finishing off a language session prior to moving the pupils to another activity. Penny turned to Tanya and began an interaction based on the activity change. Tanya responded with a slight smile as Penny began the interaction, and continued participating in the interaction with Penny for the next five minutes, fussing on several occasions when Penny had to leave her to deal with another pupil, but quieting immediately Penny spoke to her again.

With both Clive and Tanya, Penny used her knowledge of the individual to pick a moment when an interaction was likely to be successful because the child was in an alert state (described by staff in Tanya's case as 'listening') but not absorbed in an activity. Penny's ongoing monitoring of the behaviour of those pupils in her class whom she was not currently working with individually enabled her to capitalise on their readiness for interaction.

Ann also uses her knowledge of her pupils to pick the appropriate moment to start an interaction. In Figure 4.1a Emma is quiet and alert. This is a good moment to start and Emma is soon engaged in a game with Ann (Figure 4.1b). In Figure 4.2 Sonia's head is up and her eyes wide open, indicating that she is available for interaction; again this would be a good moment to start. By contrast, when Sonia is not available, her eyes appear half-closed and her head is down.

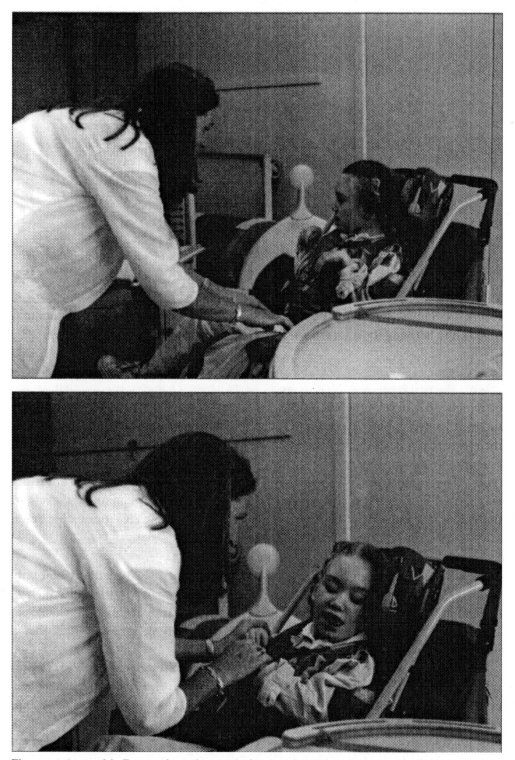

Figure 4.1a and b Emma is quiet and alert and ready to play with Ann

Figure 4.2 Sonya's 'listening' posture is characteristic of the active alert state that means she is ready for interaction

At a more global level, particularly with those people who function at an extremely early developmental level, their overall state of alertness is important for successful interactions. A number of researchers working with young babies and their caregivers have demonstrated that the baby is most likely to respond to attempts to start a 'conversation' when (like Emma and Sonia) they are alert but quiet. The importance of picking such a moment for interaction is further emphasised by research which suggests that at very early developmental levels an individual may only spend perhaps ten minutes each hour in this quiet, alert state.

Exercise
Make a list of the four or five individuals you work with most regularly and note beside each name the things that make getting their attention difficult, such as continuous behaviours or frequently being withdrawn into themselves, then note any behaviours or changes in behaviour which you think act as signals that a particular individual is ready to interact.

Ideally, then, when you want to gain the attention of someone with PMLD, you would monitor their behaviour for some indication that their attention was available to be caught (even if only briefly) and then try and engage that attention, perhaps by saying their name and pausing. However, it is not always possible to wait until someone's attention is available before you try to interact with them, so you also need strategies for making that attention available.

If you are coordinating a group working through this book together, suggest that group members observe each other's interactions with clients and note **positive** examples of interactions being started successfully through an appropriate moment being chosen for the initial approach. If your group members are to find this exercise a non-threatening and useful experience, you will need to be particularly careful to ensure that all the examples given are positive.

One way of introducing the exercise would be to give one or two examples yourself, building on the parallels drawn between the people the group are working with and the examples given earlier.

This would also be a good point to remind the group of the benefits to be derived from their differential knowledge of and skill with different clients (see Chapter 2).

You will also need to prepare for the meeting where the group are to report their observations of each other by ensuring that you have noted at least one example of an interaction being started successfully by choosing an appropriate moment for each staff member in your group, so that you are able to ensure that everyone gets some positive feedback.

Excuse me! – Interrupting attention concentrated elsewhere

In our everyday interactions, we have a number of alternative strategies for obtaining another person's attention, when they are apparently absorbed in something else. For example, we may cough, shuffle or clear our throat. All these actions, like saying someone's name, serve the function of interrupting their concentration, and making their attention available to be directed towards us, just as it is when they themselves have paused for a moment.

These strategies may not be effective with people with PMLD for two reasons; they contain an element of social learning, and they may not be sufficiently salient. However, there are some simple strategies that can be useful for getting and holding the attention of someone with PMLD, especially when you need to interact with them for some functional purpose, such as taking them to another room or helping them get ready to go home.

These strategies include exaggeration (which is parallel to the additional emphasis we may put on someone's name when our first attempt to attract their attention has failed), touching the individual you are addressing, getting eye contact (techniques that are also used in everyday interactions) and using a significant object. Findings from caregiver-infant interaction research suggest that exaggeration may be a particularly effective strategy for gaining the attention of someone who is operating at a very early developmental level. The example that follows shows staff using a combination of these techniques (with a particular emphasis on exaggeration) to gain the attention of a boy who spent much of his time engaged in stereotyped behaviour.

Tommy – interrupting stereotyped behaviour

Gaining the attention of someone who is engaged in stereotyped behaviour in order to begin an interaction can be particularly difficult. Tommy, a boy in one of the project classes, spent much of his time absorbed in watching his own hand-flapping. However, the staff who worked with him regularly had become skilled in a range of appropriate ways of breaking into his self-absorption so that his attention was briefly available to be caught.

Richard, Tommy's teacher, wanting to engage him in a group 'good morning' song, spoke and signed in a slow and exaggerated way, at the same time moving his face close to Tommy's. Using this method, Richard was successful in breaking Tommy's concentration on his hand-flapping. Tommy continued to attend to the singing for several minutes.

On another occasion, an assistant, Jean, needed Tommy's attention. First, she said his name and tapped him gently on the arm. When this was unsuccessful, like Richard, she spoke slowly in a louder than normal voice, and moved her face close to Tommy's. Tommy's self-absorption was broken for a split second, but Jean did not succeed in capturing his attention, so she moved to a position where she was directly in Tommy's line of vision and repeated her greeting. This time she was successful in starting an interaction; Tommy looked at her and smiled.

A few minutes later, Jean offered Tommy a drink, and when he apparently gave no response, she tapped the cup gently on the table, moving it into Tommy's visual field as she did so. Tommy's attention was caught by this strategy, and Jean was able to offer him a choice of drinks.

This example shows that exaggeration can take a number of forms. Jean and Richard both slowed down their speech and moved their faces closer to Tommy's and Richard made unusually large signing movements. Both Jean and Richard also spoke slightly more loudly than usual, and they could also have made their voices more emphatic. These exaggerations both made Jean and Richard's attempts more salient, and therefore more likely to attract Tommy's attention and gave him more time to respond to them.

Figure 4.3 shows Penny attracting Ben's attention by touching his arm and using an exaggerated facial expression. Ann has her face very close to Leanne when first trying to catch her attention (Figure 4.4), and Leanne's subsequent

Figure 4.3 Catching Ben's attention

Figure 4.4 Ann has her face very close to Leanne when first trying to catch her attention

engagement in the peek-a-boo game (see Figure 3.4) shows that she was successful. Another successful exaggeration staff used with Emma was to lengthen the first syllable of her name and make the second very definite: 'E.........m ma!'

Other ways of increasing salience

Sometimes even exaggeration of the sort that Jean and Richard used successfully with Tommy is not sufficient to attract the attention of someone who is very self-absorbed. In such circumstances it can be useful to emphasise your own features using things such as face paints or glitter. Figure 4.5 shows Penny successfully catching Katie's attention by putting a glittery decoration (which is being used as part of a group game) on her head. Although Katie is still holding the rattle in which she has been absorbed in this picture, her face shows that she is, at least momentarily, paying attention to Penny.

Figure 4.5 Katie's momentary attention to Penny's 'hair'

A conversation, not a monologue

The opportunity for the other person to respond (which Richard and Jean gave Tommy by slowing down their speech) is a crucial aspect of an interaction that is a 'conversation' rather than a monologue, and also of a responsive environment.

When I began to examine the sort of environments that people with PMLD experience, one of the first discoveries I made was that other people often spoke or acted as if someone with PMLD was unlikely to respond to them. This was especially likely to happen when a member of staff had a functional purpose in initiating the interaction (such as moving the pupil concerned to a new position, getting them ready for lunch etc.) but it also happened at other times, even during conversations of which the main purpose was the conversation itself.

Of course, this sort of interaction occurs, at least in part, because holding a conversation with someone with PMLD is genuinely difficult. As in the interactions between caregivers and infants with difficulties described in Chapter 1, the exceptional slowness with which a person with PMLD may respond, and the likelihood that they will not respond as consistently as someone without difficulties, leads to an expectation that they are unlikely to respond. The other participant in the conversation may then start to behave as if they are not expecting a response and to assume a more and more dominant role in the interaction. As a consequence, fewer and fewer opportunities are provided for the person with PMLD to respond. A vicious circle is created in which lack of response from the person with PMLD creates an expectation that no responses will be forthcoming, and few opportunities for responses are given.

Of course, making sure you have the other person's attention before continuing with the conversation, by using the strategies already described in this chapter, is a big step on the way to giving them the opportunity to respond, because it is by a response of some sort that you know that you have their attention. However, you also need to ensure that you continue to give them opportunities to respond as the interaction proceeds.

If you are coordinating a group working through this book together, you need to make sure that copies of the information you compiled about individuals when looking at communicative intent (Chapter 2) are available for your next meeting. You will probably find it useful to look over these for examples of the type of responses made by different individuals before the meeting; and to read through the next section so that you can help the group identify some of the less obvious responses that individuals may make.

Fortunately, there are several easy-to-use strategies for altering your behaviour in order to give a person with PMLD more opportunities to respond.

The simplest way of indicating to someone else that it is now their turn to 'speak' is to pause in your own speech or actions. We do this naturally in conversations with people without difficulties. But pausing within a conversation in order to allow the other person a turn doesn't simply consist of not speaking. As we come to the end of what we are saying we also concentrate our attention on the other person, looking at them, and probably making eye contact. We continue to look at them as they take their turn. In the same way, when you pause for a response in your interaction with a person with PMLD, you need not just to stop but to concentrate your attention on them. You need also to remember that because, in general, a person with PMLD is likely to take longer than average to respond, you may have to pause for what seems like a long time, and this may feel very awkward, especially at first.

An additional strategy that can help you to concentrate on the person with PMLD while you are waiting for a response is to know what sort of response you might get; whether a smile, a cessation in ongoing behaviour, vocalisation, eye contact etc. The information you compiled while working through Chapter 2 is likely to contain examples of the sort of responses you can expect from the various individuals with whom you work.

However, it may also be useful to know some of the types of response that you are likely to get, especially if you are working with someone whom you don't know particularly well. Smiles, vocalisations and eye contact are things that we would all easily recognise as responses, but the response of someone who is still at a very early level of development or who, for example, has a severe visual impairment may be less obvious. For instance, one of the earliest responses to develop is a reduction in the person's overall level of behaviour. This is similar to the 'quieting' response of a young baby on being picked up by a familiar adult. If someone has a severe visual impairment, they may respond not with their face, but with their hands (Fraiberg 1977; RNIB 1995); so while it may often be sensible to concentrate your attention on someone's face when you are expecting a response, you need to be aware of the other ways in which particular individuals may respond.

In the Contingency-Sensitive Environments Project we observed the extent to which staff paused to give pupils the opportunity to respond. We found that some pupils, mainly those with the most severe difficulties, got comparatively few opportunities to respond. Staff taking part in the project found that a useful way of learning to pause sufficiently for pupils to respond was to select one of these individuals who got the fewest opportunities and make a conscious effort to pause for a response during one particular activity. Using this method staff quickly increased the extent to which they gave all pupils the opportunity to respond. They found (as we have consistently found in our research) that when they did this the person with PMLD participated in the interaction more frequently and this made them more satisfying to be with.

Organisational strategies

Organisational strategies may also be useful in ensuring people get a chance to respond. For example, the 'active support' procedures described by Jones *et al.*

(1999) may have been successful in increasing the engagement of people with severe and profound disabilities in daily living activities because the graduated system of prompts employed ensured that staff waited for a response before moving on to the next level of prompting.

Exercise

Observing whether or not someone gives their conversational partner opportunities to respond is quite simple: you simply have to look for pauses in which they concentrate their attention on their partner, and conversely for times when you would expect such pauses to occur in normal conversation and they do not. Whether you are reading this book as an individual or are part of a group working through it together, you may be able to organise a situation where you video some of your own interactions to watch later, by leaving a video camera running for part of the day in much the same way as was suggested in Chapter 3. You don't need good pictures for this, and you don't need anyone to operate the camera; much of the video we used for the research project was collected by leaving the camera on a chair facing the individual we wanted to film, so any borrowed video camera which can be placed safely where it can 'see' at least part of the room where you will be working will do. If this is possible, look at a few minutes of video, concentrating on picking out occasions when you did pause to allow the person you were working with to respond, especially those occasions when it was particularly difficult to do so (for example, if you had to move one person in order to work with another or were in a hurry). Remember not to be too hard on yourself; we often fail to give others long enough to respond in our everyday interactions with our family and friends. These examples from video taken during the research project should help you to do this. They also show how all activities from the most mundane to the more exotic can be made into conversations.

Kim and Cliff: Chances to respond during an everyday activity

Kim has already told Clifford that he is going to have a drink, and that she is going to fetch a choice of drinks for him.

As she returns Cliff looks towards her.

She responds, 'I've got you one.'

Kim offers Cliff a choice of 'milk or orange'.

She speaks slowly and distinctly and moves the item she's talking about slightly.

This gives Cliff the opportunity to respond

Which he does, first by lifting his head slightly and then by looking at the juice.

Kim now wants Cliff to help in pouring the juice into the cup. She takes his hand and begins to move it towards the jug and only then tells him, 'Except that you have to help pour it. Hold the handle.'

(He doesn't really get a chance to respond and pulls away slightly.)

Kim tells Cliff, 'Look at what we're doing.'

Again he gets a chance to respond

And does so appropriately.

It is noticeable from this sequence that Kim uses some of the same techniques for attracting Cliff's attention as Jean and Richard used with Tommy. It is also noticeable that when Kim did not give Cliff the chance to respond before putting his hand on the jug handle, he responded negatively. I have repeatedly found in my research that when people are given the chance to respond, they are more likely to respond positively, whereas when they not given this opportunity they are more likely to respond negatively (Ware 1990, 1994).

Linda and Mary: Giving opportunities to respond to someone with very severe difficulties

Linda is making bread with Mary.

Linda pushes Mary's hands onto the dough repeating in a sing-song voice, 'Mary press the dough'. **She pauses** but there is no response from Mary.

Linda stops again and says 'Mary do it' and **pauses**.

Linda repeats 'Mary do it' and **pauses again**.

Linda takes Mary's hands and demonstrates.

Linda sings 'Mary press the dough' as she herself is banging it. **She pauses** again.

Linda demonstrates with Mary's hands again and says 'Oh, it's lovely and warm.' **She pauses again** but still there is no response from Mary.

Linda rolls up the dough and says 'Shall we have another go?' Mary looks briefly at Linda (in response?) and Linda looks closely into her face.

Linda presses Mary's hands gently in the dough again and **pauses**.

Mary looks at Linda.

Linda responds: 'Don't look at me' in a teasing voice.

In this interaction Linda persists over several minutes in pausing to give Mary the chance to respond and eventually Mary does so. A situation in which the person you are working with does not noticeably respond despite repeated opportunities is one in which it is particularly difficult to continue to pause for responses. It would have been very easy for Linda to give up, and simply physically manipulate Mary's hands in the dough. Additionally, although Linda is asking Mary to 'press the dough', because that is what the activity demands, she is prepared to accept any response from Mary because she knows that Mary's repertoire of behaviours is very limited. In the next chapter I look at some of the strategies you can use to encourage a response in situations like this.

Ben: Looking for responses during physio sessions

Ben, like Mary, has very severe difficulties, and his ability to make physical responses is extremely limited. Like many people with PMLD he needs regular physio/exercise sessions to ensure he retains as wide a range of movement as possible and doesn't experience unnecessary discomfort from contractures etc. Of course, many of the exercises the physio has prescribed for Ben involve passive movements, and it would be especially easy in this situation not to give Ben any opportunities to respond.

Figures 4.6a and 4.6b show how, although she carefully carries out the full range of exercises the physio believes Ben requires, Penny repeatedly gives Ben opportunities to respond, by doing the exercises slowly, pausing and keeping herself constantly in a position where she will observe any response Ben makes.

If you are coordinating a group working through this book together, you may like to invite volunteers to bring a short piece of video of themselves interacting with someone who they find it difficult to engage in interaction. Ask the group to watch the video through once and identify examples of times when the staff member concerned did give the pupil/client the opportunity to respond and also any changes in behaviour which might be interpreted as a response. Emphasise the things that the volunteer is already doing that should be contributing to a successful interaction (even if they don't appear to be working!). Finally ask the group for suggestions as to how these aspects can be extended and capitalised on. For instance, someone who is using some exaggeration with limited success could be encouraged to exaggerate more as in the examples in this chapter. Remind the group of the ground rules for watching video of each other before you start. (Where someone hasn't responded to a behaviour, it's probably because they didn't see it or didn't appreciate its significance. Positive examples are better than negative ones – so suggest ways in which the person can extend what they are doing well already rather than listing the times they missed opportunities.) People may prefer to do this exercise in pairs of their own choosing.

Figures 4.6a and 4.6b Penny pauses and watches for a response from Ben during a physio/exercise session

Summary

In this chapter I have described a number of strategies that should enable you to maximise your chances of being successful in initiating an interaction with an individual with PMLD by:

• Being aware of the signals that indicate that an individual's attention is available.

- Having a variety of strategies for catching and holding their attention.
- Knowing what strategies may work when you need to interrupt an individual's attention to an activity in order to engage them in some other way.
- Signalling clearly that you wish to have a conversation with them especially by allowing sufficient pauses for them to respond and keeping your attention focused on their likely response.
- Giving them practice at 'conversations' by making sure that every activity (including those that are purely functional) provides opportunities for reciprocal interactions.

Being aware of when it is appropriate to end the interaction is also important and you need to be aware of signals the individual may use which show you that they have had enough for the time being, or that they wish the interaction to continue when you stop. These issues are dealt with in the next chapter.

CHAPTER 5

Sharing Control

The last two chapters have been concerned with specific aspects of interactions: responding in Chapter 3 and initiating in Chapter 4. In this chapter I look at the overall framework of the interaction. I examine:

- how you can keep a conversation going;
- how you can structure the conversation to give the other person opportunities to take the initiative;
- how you can help the other person to be an equal partner in the interaction;
- how you can know whether or not the other person wants the interaction to continue.

In Chapter 1 I described how, in both everyday conversations between friends, and in interactions between caregivers and infants, the participants take turns to speak or act and the lead in the interaction passes from one to the other. The opportunity to participate equally in interactions is vital for two reasons: it facilitates communicative and cognitive development, and it provides the opportunity for raising self-esteem.

Keeping the conversation going

In many of the conversations I have observed between staff in various roles and the people with PMLD with whom they work, the staff member frequently fills in the other person's turn and also takes the leading role virtually all the time.

For example, when a pupil returns to school after the weekend in a new sweatshirt I have sometimes heard a conversation something like this:

'That's a nice sweatshirt, Mary, it's new isn't it? I must say, red really suits you and is that a bird on it? Oh, I see it's an owl! – I bet you got it from your brother's club – Tim goes to young ornithologists, doesn't he?'

Or like this:

> 'What did you do at the weekend, Vijay? — Mum says you went to Southall market with Dad. And you got that new sweatshirt there. Did Dippi go too? I see, she stayed at home with mum.'

It's difficult to convey the feel of these 'conversations' in writing, without appearing to caricature them; because, of course, there's more to a conversation than words. But, in the first case, the member of staff is giving a running commentary on Mary's sweatshirt rather than talking to Mary about it. Mary is given little chance to join in, partly because the commentary proceeds without any real pauses; but also because, although superficially there are places where you might expect a response from Mary, in fact the commentary isn't really structured to allow her the opportunity to respond. You can get some idea of how this might feel from Mary's perspective by reading the commentary out loud, without really pausing for breath.

The second example is very similar, except that here the staff member supplies both sides of the conversation, rather than giving a running commentary. Perhaps the member of staff does not expect Vijay to respond, so answers for him with the help of his home-school diary. The key issue is that, like the first example, the conversation isn't really structured to facilitate Vijay's responding. Again, you can get the idea by reading it aloud.

Of course, it's not surprising that conversations of this type take place, when you consider that in terms of communicative competence, both Mary and Vijay may be functioning like young children, although physically they may be young adults. Indeed 'pseudo-dialogues' like these represent reasonable attempts by the staff member to keep the conversation going in difficult circumstances. Unfortunately, though, interactions of this sort aren't likely to help people with PMLD to learn more sophisticated communication skills. So, how is it possible to interact with someone whose cognitive development may be very much at odds with their physical development in a way that encourages them to develop their communication skills?

When one of the participants in an interaction is much more competent than the other, it's natural for the more competent communicator to lead the interaction. When an adult interacts with a young baby, they initially control the structure and direction of the interaction. Infants without difficulties gradually come to assume a more equal role in interactions, because adults are skilled at enabling them to participate. In particular, as I discussed in Chapter 2, caregivers attribute meaning to all sorts of behaviours that the baby does not intend as communications, accepting these as the baby's contributions to the interaction. Additionally, the caregiver structures their own conversational turn so that it is both a response to what the infant has just done and an invitation to the infant to make another response.

'Turnabouts'

Responses like this, consisting of a reaction to the other person's turn and a further invitation to them to take another turn in the conversation (called 'turnabouts'[1]), are characteristic not just of caregivers' efforts to continue a conversation with a young baby but of interactions between adults, and between adults and infants who are beginning to develop more sophisticated communication skills. Only when a number of attempts have received no response from the infant does the caregiver pretend that the infant has taken a turn or fill in their turn for them. However, when a child (or adult) has learning difficulties they are less likely to do something that the other person involved in the conversation can construe as a turn. How can you make it more likely that they will do so?

In the last chapter I talked about the importance of pausing with your attention on the other person, demonstrating that you are expecting a response, and being alert to any behaviour that can be interpreted as that response. In addition to pauses, the fact that you are expecting the other person to respond can be indicated by 'turnabouts'. However, these are comparatively rare in interactions in which one of the participants has severe or profound learning difficulties. As represented above, the staff member's contributions to the 'conversation' with Mary are unlikely to encourage her to respond. However, there are two places where a slight restructuring of the adult's contribution would enable a turnabout to be used in a natural manner. (These are represented below by italics, with the comment on Mary's previous action in normal type, while the new topic is in bold type.)

'That's a nice sweatshirt, Mary, it's new isn't it? *I must say, red really suits you* **and is that a bird on it?** *Oh, I see it's an owl!* – I bet you got it from your brother's club – **Tim goes to young ornithologists, doesn't he?**'

To capitalise on these opportunities the conversation might be restructured like this

Staff Member	*Mary*
That's a nice sweatshirt, Mary. Is it new? **Pause**	
	[Does not respond]
I must say, red really suits you! **and is that a bird on it?** **Pause**	
	gurgles

---

[1]   The term 'turnabout' was coined by Kaye and Charney (1981).

Oh, I see it's an owl!
– I bet you got it
from your brother's club
– *Tim goes to young*
ornithologists, doesn't he?
Pause

smiles

Mary's turns in this conversation consist of very simple responses but, nonetheless, despite Mary's initial failure to make any response, the staff member's skill engages her in an interaction which has a conversational structure. In addition to the turnabouts with their accompanying pauses, the direct question 'Is it new?' gets the conversation off on the right foot, because it's natural to follow it with a pause. This interaction is appropriate both developmentally (because its structure allows any response that Mary makes to be incorporated into the conversation) and chronologically (because a conversation about a new sweatshirt could take place with someone of any age).

By contrast, the conversation with Vijay contains no turnabouts and although superficially questions are being asked of him, in fact, the staff member responds for him. Nonetheless, with some slight restructuring this conversation too could offer real opportunities for Vijay to participate while still capitalising on the information supplied in the home-school diary.

Staff member	*Vijay*
What did you do at the weekend, Vijay?	
Pause	
	®
You went to Southall market with Dad?	
Pause	
	®
And you got that new sweatshirt there.	
Did Dippi go too?	
Pause	
	®
I see, she stayed at home with mum.	

In this version of the conversation, the pauses allow anything that Vijay does (represented by the ®s in the dialogue above) to be interpreted as his turn in the conversation and the turnabout (italicised) enables the conversational structure to continue with a new topic.

Of course, in both these examples, the probability that Mary or Vijay will participate partly depends on whether the staff member is successful in engaging Mary or Vijay's attention through the techniques described in Chapter 4.

If you are coordinating a group working through this book together, you will need to read through the examples of turnabouts given below and the exercise that follows well before the session in order to be able to give examples that are directly relevant to your situation.

The examples that follow illustrate staff from the project classes using turnabouts in a variety of situations to keep interactions going.

Chris and Nayake

Nayake and Dawn have been sat alongside each other by Paddy ready for Chris to work with them:

Chris says, 'Hello girls, are you all ready?' **Pause**

'Are you all ready and waiting?' **Pause**

Nayake begins to smile and move her mouth.

Chris responds, 'Oh that's nice.' **Pause**

Nayake smiles more broadly and begins to vocalise.

Chris responds: 'You were, were you? *What did Paddy say? Did she say sit there and wait for Chris?*' **Pause**

Nayake vocalises loudly, her face wreathed in smiles.

Chris says: 'She did, did she?'

In the italicised turnabout Chris acknowledges Nayake's smiling and vocalisation as if Nayake had told her what she had been doing, which facilitates the continuation of the conversation, and Nayake's next response is also incorporated as if she had confirmed Chris's statement.

Penny and Tanya

Penny has started Tanya's physiotherapy, and Elaine is shortly to take over to complete the exercises. The early exercises are ones that Tanya enjoys and she giggles constantly; but Penny then has to do some exercises that Tanya does not enjoy, and Tanya shouts in protest.

Tanya:	Shouts
Penny:	'Out and flat!'
Tanya:	Shouts

Penny:	*'Listen!* **I don't think that Elaine will want to deal with you.'**
Tanya:	Shouts
Penny:	'No, she won't.'
Tanya:	Laughs
Penny:	'No, she possibly won't.'

The turnabout (italicised) enables Penny to treat Tanya's protesting as turns in the conversation; as a consequence Tanya stops protesting and joins in.

By treating the other person's action as a 'turn' in an ongoing conversation, turnabouts such as these enable a conversation to take place where otherwise there might have been no mutual interaction. (See also the example of Suzanne's conversation with Susannah on page 83.)

Exercise

Identify a person with whom you carry out a particular activity on a regular basis; for example, you might regularly do an aromatherapy session with someone, or be responsible for helping them prepare a drink. Arrange to position a video camera where it can 'see' the session. After the session review the video noting what you did that the person responded to, your own responses to what they did and whether you used any turnabouts (you may find it helpful to write down the interaction in the format given above for Mary and Vijay). The idea of this exercise is to help you become more aware of how you can respond to the people you work with in ways that promote interactions whose structure resembles a conversation. Before your next session with this individual, identify ways in which using a turnabout would have enhanced the interaction and then repeat the exercise on the next occasion you work with this individual. For example, during an aromatherapy session, you might have invited the client to have a sniff of the oil. Perhaps they smile. You might decide that you could introduce a turnabout at this point by responding *'Hm, it does smell really nice, doesn't it? Do you want some on your hands?'* If you are unable to arrange access to video you might be able to carry out this exercise by ensuring that you have time to write down and review what happened immediately after the session. If you select this method, you should choose a short interaction, such as that which takes place when somebody arrives with you for a particular session. However, I would strongly advocate that you use video for this exercise since you are much more likely to see subtle responses, and be able to work out if you could have incorporated these by using turnabouts, if you have the opportunity to watch the interaction in a quiet environment. Alternatively, you may be able to ask a colleague to carry out an observation for you (see coordinator's box below).

If you are coordinating a group working through this book together, try and arrange for video of each member of the group for a session of their choice. In reviewing these video extracts, members of the group might help each other identify places where additional turnabouts could be incorporated, after first commenting on positive aspects of the interaction. If using video is difficult in your situation, you can carry out this exercise by asking members of the group to observe each other, identify places where turnabouts were used and suggest places where additional turnabouts might have been incorporated. Whichever version of the exercise you are using, you will need to repeat the instructions about the need to make positive comments to others about their interactions which you gave for the exercise in Chapter 4.

Letting the other person take the lead

Turnabouts can be used to continue the conversation, not only after the other person has responded to your initiation, but in response to an initiation from them which may or may not be connected to the previous 'topic' of conversation.

Thus, when a caregiver speaks to a young infant, anything the infant does, from waving his or her arms to yawning, will be interpreted as a response. For instance, the yawn may get the response from the caregiver, 'Oh, I'm boring you am I, well, what would you like to talk about?'

This type of response, of course, leaves the way open for the interaction to continue, since the next thing that the infant does can be interpreted by the caregiver as a new topic of conversation. In this way, not only is the interaction potentially continued, but the initiative is passed to the infant.

Often when you are talking to a friend or partner, perhaps trying to get a decision on what to eat for tea tonight, they are distracted, for example by something they remember they want to tell you or by an external event such as an unusual car passing outside the window. When this happens you may either follow their new train of thought before returning to the original topic, or try to get them to ignore the distraction. Sometimes an interaction will include many diversions of this sort.

Similarly when someone with PMLD makes an initiation which is apparently unconnected with what you see as the purpose of the interaction, it is possible to either follow their lead or try to continue with your original purpose. Obviously it isn't always appropriate to follow such diversions, but doing so has the advantage of handing over control of the interaction to the other person, even if only briefly.

Researchers trying to help caregivers of children with difficulties to be less dominant in interactions with them have found that asking the caregiver to follow the child's interest helps to achieve this.

Sharing control is difficult for teachers but vital for children

It is, perhaps, especially difficult to relax control if you are a teacher, whether by profession or because your job definition includes teaching. There may be comparatively few occasions when you interact with your pupils/clients without having a particular purpose in mind. Often, you feel pressurised to achieve your goal and move on to the next task. Staff in other situations, too, will usually have a specific reason for interacting with the people with PMLD for whom they are responsible, whether it is teaching a particular skill or initiating a leisure activity.

This contrasts with our interactions with our friends for which we often have no specific goal. Even with our work colleagues an interaction that begins for a particular purpose, for example arranging the time of a meeting, often changes into one that is less goal-oriented. Having agreed to the meeting, your colleague may well introduce an unrelated topic of discussion such as last night's television programmes, the cricket scores or the local news. Someone who has PMLD may well lack many of the skills required for moving an interaction from a functional purpose to a pleasurable one. This means that those who work with them have to be especially alert to possibilities for allowing them to steer the direction of the interaction.

For example, Jill, a teacher in one of the project classes, was working with Ranvir trying to get her to grasp some bells that were suspended above her. Ranvir, however, was distracted by the patterns made by the sun shining through the window. Jill stopped, looked in the same direction as Ranvir and asked, 'What are you looking at? Is the sun making pretty patterns?' Thus, she implicitly acknowledges Ranvir's interest in the patterns and allows it briefly to control the interaction.

In this interaction, Ranvir's interest in the patterns made by the sunshine is an unplanned event on which Jill capitalises.

In a similar, unplanned way Beatrice (a teenager with profound learning difficulties but some simple intentional communication) in an interaction with Ruth (a nursery nurse) takes advantage of a pause that occurs while Ruth is recording to try and grab a piece of biscuit. Ruth laughs and asks: 'Are you after some more? I think there's one more piece hiding somewhere – you have to sign for it.' Ruth has already helped Beatrice to sign biscuit, and Beatrice has already had some biscuit. Now Ruth responds to Beatrice's attempt to grab more biscuit, not with a reprimand, but as if it is a request for more. Thus, in a situation designed to teach a particular skill – signing biscuit – Ruth uses an unplanned event to enable Beatrice to take the lead.

Following the individual's interest can be made easier by providing materials in which you think they are likely to show an interest, either because they are similar to things that have attracted their interest in the past or because the materials themselves are likely to behave in novel ways.

As part of her 'tapping game' (described in detail in Chapter 6) Penny provided materials which she hoped would prove attractive to individual members of her group. Materials that attract interest in this way give opportunities to the staff involved to hand over control by following the response of the person with PMLD as if it were an initiation commenting on or asking for the materials.

Other ways of relaxing control

Following the other person's lead is fine if they do something that either does provide a new focus to the conversation (as in Jill's interaction with Ranvir) or that you can interpret as providing a new focus. However, if someone rarely seems to do this, you need other ways of encouraging them to take the lead.

Pausing

In her interaction with Beatrice, Ruth capitalised on Beatrice's response to an unplanned pause (caused by Ruth's recording). In Chapter 4 I talked about the importance of pausing as a way of encouraging the other person to respond, but pausing can also be used as a way of encouraging the other person to take over the lead. For example, Richard in an interaction with Tommy, sets up a situation where the lead can easily pass to Tommy.

Richard has already made a chocolate spread sandwich with Tommy, most of which Tommy has eaten with prompting from Richard. Now Richard is looking closely at Tommy. He says, 'Did you enjoy that chocolate spread sandwich?' and **pauses**. A few seconds later, Tommy grabs one of the remaining pieces of sandwich and **Richard responds to him:** 'Oh, he says so much so.' At this point the interaction moves to Tommy's control. Richard develops from Tommy's action, encouraging him to keep hold of the sandwich.

Waiting for the other person to start the interaction

Another important way of increasing the control experienced by the person with PMLD is to give them the opportunity to begin the interaction. On one occasion while I was in Penny's class Jenny, the music therapist, came into the classroom to fetch one of the pupils for a regular session, but instead of immediately speaking to Penny, or the child she had come to collect, she waited without speaking, both for a pause in the ongoing activity which would increase the chances of whichever child she speaks to responding to her (see Chapter 4), and to see if anyone would notice her presence and initiate an interaction. By planning collaboratively, you can capitalise on routine interruptions like this to give people the opportunity to initiate interactions in a natural context.

Imitation

In Chapter 3 I mentioned imitation as a strategy that can decrease the extent to which the more competent interactive partner dominates the interaction. When a caregiver interacts with a very young baby, one of the things they do naturally is to pick up on the baby's rhythm and insert their actions in the pauses between the baby's actions. If, in what they do, they also copy the baby's actions, this provides the baby with very positive feedback. This idea of imitating or echoing the other person's actions can be used deliberately with a person with PMLD.

Miranda and Timmy

For example, when Miranda, a young assistant with no formal training other than that provided within the research project, is part way through a 'social skills' session with Timmy, she asks him: 'Are you going to have a biscuit again?' Timmy moves his head, putting it slightly on one side and Miranda imitates him. After this sequence has been repeated several times, Timmy begins to chuckle.

In this example the imitation took place naturally within an ongoing interaction; but it is also possible to structure an interaction to include opportunities for the other person to do things that can be imitated. Imitation not only enables the other person to take the lead, it also often has the effect of slowing down the interaction, which also gives the other person more opportunity to participate.

> If you are coordinating a group working through this book together, arrange for pairs to observe each other and give feedback on *positive* aspects of interaction, i.e. things that keep it going and allow the child to take over. Remember to stress the need to give positive feedback. It would be best to carry out this observation after people have had the opportunity to do the next exercise.

Exercise

Identify a time when you are likely to be interacting with a particular person. It can be any time, for example you may be responsible for helping them prepare for work, taking them to the toilet, assisting them in preparing the dinner or numerous other activities. If possible, choose someone who you know does not communicate intentionally (see Chapter 2). Once you have initiated the interaction, try to hand over control to the other person, using one or more of the ways described in this chapter (following the other person's interests, pausing, prompting and pausing or imitation).

Encouraging more equal interactions with peers

Of course, it would be a mistake to think that the only interactions that are important are those between staff and pupils/clients. People also need opportunities to interact with their peers with and without learning difficulties.

While there is little research that examines interactions between individuals with PMLD, Landesman-Dwyer and Sackett (1978) noted that when individuals with PMLD were given the opportunity to interact with each other they engaged in mutual touching and exploring behaviours, and that individuals given these opportunities slept less and were more active than a control group. Although the Contingency-Sensitive Environments Project was not concerned with interactions with peers, we found that a number of such interactions did take place, from vocalising in response to another child vocalising to apparently deliberate touching.

Studies by Gleason (1990) suggest that prolonged social exchanges can take place between individuals with PMLD. He describes the interactions between two young men with PMLD, Danial and Thomas, on a 'total care' ward. The extract from Gleason's description which follows is included to give the flavour of the reciprocal nature of the relationship between the two young men.

A key event occurred in the ward one afternoon during rest period when the teachers and professionals who were at lunch failed to return to conduct afternoon activities.

The first attendant passes by Thomas who is on the edge of the mat pushing a blue-handled Fisher-Price lawn mower into the aisle. She says to him, 'Now, Thomas, don't be pushing that out into the aisle.' She repeats herself more emphatically as she continues to walk by Thomas.

A second attendant finds the toy in the aisle and comments to the first attendant, 'They kill for this toy.'

Danial is brought in on a bed stretcher and laid down next to Thomas. Both boys are lying on their back. A foster-grandmother picks up a second lawn mower with a white handle and places it between them. The Fisher-Price lawn mower has a wooden handle; one is white and the other is blue. The handle is attached to a plastic cylinder with coloured balls inside. When rolled across a surface, plastic wheels on either side of the cylinder turn plastic blades inside the cylinder. Coloured balls fly in all directions. The wheels engage a disc that repeats a tune over and over. When it rolls, the lawn mower displays popping coloured balls that seem to accompany the tune.

Danial swings the white-handled lawn mower over his head at a doll suspended from the ceiling. Holding it like a flag, Danial lifts the toy over his head.

An attendant sees the two boys together, picks up Thomas and says, 'Come on.' With another attendant, she brings him to another mat across the room. Hardly on the mat for a minute, Thomas starts to move across the floor.

In slow accordion-like movements, Thomas moves across the floor on his back half-inch by half-inch, a distance of 20 feet. Danial himself moves off the mat into the aisle maintaining his hold on the white-handled toy. Each boy stops his movement as the second attendant passes, glancing down and saying, 'This is their favourite toy. They all like it.'

In a series of three rolls, Danial finds himself head-to-toe with Thomas. Thomas manoeuvres himself into a position parallel to Danial. Each boy grips his toy and inches down toward the other, positioning the lawn mowers next to one another. Thomas reaches for Danial's white-handled lawn mower. Danial pulls it back. He pushes the lawn mower forward as he moves back. Thomas grabs at Danial's white handle while Danial grabs at Thomas's blue handle. Suddenly, Thomas throws himself forward and grabs the white-handled lawn mower. Danial seizes the opportunity to grab the blue-handled lawn mower and raises it about his head. Thomas turns away from Danial and rolls the white-handled lawn mower on the floor.

The initiative in this interaction passes back and forth between Danial and Thomas and is clearly one between equal partners. It is also highly routinised and engaged in by Danial and Thomas because they enjoy interaction. Gleason comments that in this situation the two young men show greater interactive skill than in 'programmed activities designed for the purpose'. The level of complexity with which they interact is dependent both on the 'right partner' being present and apparently on the appropriate equipment. As this example shows, encouraging peer interactions is another important way of increasing the opportunities that people with PMLD get to take the lead in interactions, and assume a more equal share of control for the interaction. Observations that enable you to make and test out educated guesses about the meaning of an individual's behaviours in interaction with his or her peers are just as crucial as they are in enhancing the interactions between staff and people with PMLD.

For people with PMLD in integrated environments, access to opportunities to take the lead in interactions may be particularly difficult, since the probability is that peers, like staff, are more communicatively competent and tend to dominate interactions. This issue along with other aspects of promoting a responsive environment in inclusive settings are discussed in detail in Chapter 6, while examples of using information and communication technology (ICT) to promote responsive interactions are discussed in Chapter 7.

'Push off!' or 'Don't go away yet' – being sensitive to the other person's wishes with regard to continuing the conversation

The final aspect of control relates to whether an interaction continues or ends. Often when you interact with someone with PMLD you control both the start and end of the conversation; you have come to give them a drink and when the drink is finished you leave. But it may be that though you have finished, the other person wishes the interaction to continue. Alternatively, you try and continue an interaction when the other person wants to be alone.

If you have gone to see a colleague to arrange, for example, an exchange of shifts, as you are leaving the room, having completed the business, they say, 'Oh, by the way...' This phrase and others like it act as signals that they wish the interaction to continue. Depending on the circumstances, you may pause and give them your attention or excuse yourself: 'Sorry Mary, got to rush...'

In the same way people with PMLD may well have particular behaviours that they use as signals to indicate that they wish an interaction to continue. Although, just as with a work colleague, it isn't possible to continue the interaction whenever the other person wishes to, you can be alert to the strategies that individuals use to indicate their desire to continue an interaction and acknowledge their wishes even when you have to excuse yourself.

Tanya

Tanya, who was described in Chapter 4 as often vocalising when left by a member of staff who had been interacting with her, used this behaviour as a 'repair' strategy (see Coupe O'Kane and Goldbart 1998). On one occasion two members of staff, Penny and Elaine, were giving drinks to a group of pupils. As Tanya finishes the last mouthful of her drink, Elaine says: 'Let go then, good girl, all gone.' Having released the cup from Tanya's fingers, Elaine moves away and, having asked Penny who is to have a drink next, she speaks to Clive: 'Right, would you like a cup of tea, my love?'

Meanwhile, Tanya begins to move her hands and 'shouts'. Penny interprets this as a repair strategy, comes across to her, leans on the back of her chair, and says: 'Hey, listen here you, Elaine's just given you a drink. Don't deny it, she's just given you a drink.' As Penny leans forward Tanya makes eye contact. Penny then turns away to give a drink to Rosie, who is sitting next to Tanya. After being quiet for a short while, Tanya starts shouting again. Although Penny is occupied with giving Rosie her drink, she responds to Tanya again, saying: 'No, you've had a drink, you'll just have to wait a few minutes.' When Tanya continues shouting Penny briefly comes over to her and says, 'You've had a drink, you h-a-v-e to w-a-i-t.' Tanya smiles. When Penny has to go to the other side of the room to attend to another child who is unwell, Tanya shouts louder and louder.

Clive

Clive, who was also mentioned in the last chapter, had very profound learning difficulties and physical disabilities. On one occasion when Penny was doing Clive's physio, she had to leave him briefly. While she was gone he began to move his mouth, and these movements appeared to diminish when she returned. It is not clear that these movements were intended as a repair strategy, they may have been a reaction to Penny no longer moving his limbs, but they could be treated as if they were intended to indicate that Clive wished the interaction to continue, particularly if they were observed on other occasions as a member of staff left him.

Tanya has clear strategies for attempting to repair interactions that have been broken off, and when she is initially unsuccessful she persists in her attempts. With Clive on the other hand, it is far less clear whether his behaviour when left is an attempt to repair the interaction.

This illustrates the importance of being aware of the strategies that individuals have for repairing interactions, so that you are in a position to respond. A first step in identifying these strategies would be to use a similar procedure to that detailed in Chapter 2 for initiations. However, for some individuals it may be necessary to use more structured methods, such as the observational assessment devised by Goldbart (1994). Obviously, it is often not possible to continue an interaction, but the individual's desire that it should can be acknowledged.

> If you are coordinating a group working through this book together, you need to set aside some time in your group meetings to discuss the examples and begin to identify the strategies used by people with whom you work. For this exercise it is a good idea to start by looking at an individual who communicates in fairly clear ways. You may also need to make time for observations of those individuals whose strategies for repairing interactions are not known to the group.

Exercise

Choose one of the individuals with whom you work (preferably someone who communicates fairly clearly) and identify the strategies they use to repair interactions. Next time you are working with that individual, plan time to respond to any repair strategies that are used as you leave. Repeat this exercise with an individual whose ways of communicating are less obvious.

Recognising when someone wants to end an interaction

When we are involved in a conversation that we wish to end, we all have strategies for escaping such as: 'Gosh, is that the time? Must dash!' or, less obviously, 'Right, I'll see to that.' If the other person involved seems oblivious to these social signals that we want the conversation to end, we may get irritated (or alternatively desperate!). For example, on one occasion we had a visitor who seemed just not to notice despite a succession of signals that on this occasion he had outstayed his welcome. After trying the more usual signals – 'Well it's been really nice seeing you... We'll be in touch when we've had a chance to talk it over...' I eventually got to my feet – a clear signal that I believed he was about to leave.

Such difficulties are comparatively rare in dealing with your work or leisure acquaintances. When you are interacting with someone with PMLD, however, you can easily miss or ignore their signals that they have had enough of you for the time being. But allowing the other person to control when the interaction finishes is one way of showing our respect for them, and particularly important when the person cannot walk away. Additionally, being able to indicate that you want an interaction to finish is an essential part of learning to communicate.

One way in which some people indicate that they wish to finish an interaction is by turning away or avoiding eye contact. For example, Mary (who was mentioned in Chapter 4) sometimes turned her head away during an interaction. This happened at times that suggested that she might be trying to terminate the interaction, when she was bounced vigorously on someone's knee for some time, for example.

Another way in which someone may indicate that they wish an interaction to end is by the way in which they respond. They may respond less intensely or stop responding altogether.

Instead of necessarily making your own initiations more intense when someone does this, you need to consider whether they are trying to end the interaction. Damien, who was mentioned in Chapter 2, sometimes cast his eyes downwards, either when someone tried to initiate an interaction or during an ongoing interaction. Experienced staff who watched the video we made with him interpreted this as a signal that he wanted to terminate the interaction. Like Mary, Damien probably wasn't intentionally signalling that he wanted to end the interaction; rather his response to a situation he was not enjoying was interpreted to mean this. However, the fact that people easily agreed about the meaning of this behaviour created the potential for him to be given a degree of control.

Some people, of course, have more extreme ways of showing that they want an interaction to stop; for example Beatrice, who was mentioned earlier in this chapter, would try to push the other person away, and if this failed she screamed at them. Such extreme signals may sometimes develop when more low-key indications have not been recognised.

Susannah

Sometimes, someone 'switching off' or failing to respond can be an indication not that they want to end the interaction, but that they don't like a particular activity.

Communication aims for Susannah, whom I mentioned in Chapter 2, included increasing her vocalisations, and that she would vocalise for 'more' of an activity. During individual language sessions with Susannah, Suzanne had scheduled a variety of activities intended to meet these aims including playing 'Round and round the garden'.

On one occasion when Susannah's mother had recently had a baby, Suzanne began the language session in the normal way with a brief introductory chat and then proceeded to play 'Round and round the garden' with Susannah:

Suzanne: Is it good fun at home with your new baby?

Susannah: Looks at Suzanne

Suzanne: Hm, are you ready, are you ready, Susannah? Can I have your hand? (Gently takes Susannah's hand) **PAUSE**

Suzanne: I'm round here, look at me.

Susannah: Looks at Suzanne

Suzanne: Are you ready? Here we go!

Susannah: Looks at Suzanne

Suzanne: Round and round the garden like a teddy bear

Susannah: Vocalises and continues to look at Suzanne

Suzanne: One step, two step, and tickle Susannah there (tickles).

Susannah: Orients towards Suzanne, but casts eyes down

Suzanne: **PAUSE** What do you think, shall we do it again? **PAUSE**

Susannah: Drops head further down

Suzanne: Do you want more? **PAUSE**

Susannah: Drops head further down

Suzanne: **PAUSE** Susannah, more? **PAUSE**

Susannah: Looks up

Suzanne: Hello! **PAUSE** No, you don't want any more, shall we chat instead? Susannah, listen to this. I was sorting out my school journey yesterday **PAUSE** And I thought you might like to come with us.

Susannah: Vocalises and smiles

Suzanne: Oh would you? **PAUSE**

Susannah: Vocalises

Suzanne: Do you think your mum would let you?

Susannah: Vocalises, smiles, looks at Suzanne

Suzanne: Yes? I hope so.

By responding sensitively to Susannah's indication that she did not want to play 'Round and round the garden' and introducing an alternative activity, Suzanne was able to keep the interaction going in a way that was pleasurable for both of them, and partially achieve the objective set for the session which was for Susannah to increase her vocalisations.

Summary

In this chapter I have looked at ways in which interactions with people with PMLD can become more equal. Three aspects of sharing control of the interaction have been discussed.

- Keeping the conversation going by using initiations which are also responses to the other person's turn (turnabouts) and which enable you to accept any behaviour as a response.
- Enabling the other person to take the lead by following their interest, and by careful use of pauses and imitation.
- Responding to the other person's desire to continue or end an interaction by being aware of their strategies for indicating this.

In addition I briefly indicated some ways in which equal interactions with peers can be encouraged. In the next chapter I examine ways in which responsive interactions can be encouraged in inclusive settings and how people can be helped to become more competent communicators.

CHAPTER 6

Moving On and Moving Out

Making interaction more enjoyable for everyone concerned and teaching people that they are valued and respected as individuals are two very important reasons for creating a responsive environment; but at the same time, we want to help people with PMLD to become more competent communicators and to develop both socially and cognitively. Since the first edition of this book was published, it has become more usual for people with PMLD to spend some of their time in community settings or with their less disabled peers. This chapter is concerned with:

- how a responsive environment can be created in inclusive settings;
- how you can use the responsive environment to promote social, communicative and cognitive progress.

Creating a responsive environment in inclusive settings

There are very few published accounts of the experiences of people with PMLD in inclusive settings. One possible reason for this is that in practice very few people with PMLD spend all their time in such settings. Indeed a recent Mencap study found that pupils with PMLD were unlikely to be included in mainstream classes. For them, the most common form of inclusion was in class with peers with SLD (Mencap 1999). Julian (2002) confirms this finding. She did not find any pupils with PMLD who were included full-time in a mainstream class. What she did find was that schools in England and Wales used a wide variety of arrangements to facilitate the inclusion of pupils with PMLD. Julian's study suggests that schools are using a carefully thought out mixture of separate and inclusive provision to try and ensure 'the best of both worlds' for their pupils.

Because of the lack of evidence specifically about the experiences of people with PMLD, we need to try and extrapolate from studies of people with less severe disabilities. Even here, relatively few studies examine interaction, as opposed to other aspects of inclusive environments, and even those studies that do look at interaction rarely look specifically at the nature of interactions between people with severe disabilities and their less disabled and non-disabled peers.

Interactions with staff

At first sight, there appears to be no reason why interactions between staff and pupils with PMLD in inclusive settings should differ from those in separate provision. In general, studies of staff:pupil interactions in inclusive settings seem to confirm the view that, just as in separate environments (see Chapter 2), staff are likely to dominate the interaction. For example, this was one finding of a study by Bang and Lamb (1996) of the long-term inclusion of students with a variety of severe disabilities in a mainstream high school. It seems then as if at least some of the problems in creating a responsive environment for people with PMLD are similar regardless of the setting in which you work. So, if you work in an inclusive setting (whether full-time, or visiting with an individual or group), it should be possible to tackle these problems by taking the measures described in the previous chapters and so create a responsive environment for your pupils/clients.

However, there are also a number of differences between inclusive and separate settings which may make it more difficult for staff to be responsive in inclusive situations. First, if inclusion is part-time, there may be a number of staff who are unfamiliar with the people with PMLD. The evidence I've discussed in the previous chapters suggests that familiarity can be an important part of interpreting and responding to an individual's behaviour appropriately and consistently.

Second, in my own previous research (Ware 1987, 1990), I have found that the amount of staff time pupils receive is related to their degree of difficulty, with more disabled pupils in a class tending to receive less staff time. Jones *et al.* (1999) reports similar findings in small community houses for adults with severe and profound learning difficulties. However, what research there is suggests that pupils who are educated with less-disabled peers or peers without disabilities generally seem to spend more rather than less time interacting with staff than those peers (e.g. Cole and Meyer 1991; Julian 2002). This may be because they often have an assistant assigned specifically to them, and much of their interaction may be with that specific individual (e.g. Bang and Lamb 1996). Indeed, Cole and Meyer found that children with severe disabilities integrated into mainstream settings spent more time with teaching assistants than peers with similar disabilities in separate settings. However, this may mean that people with PMLD spend much of their time in interactions that are dominated by the other partner, and that limit their opportunities for interacting with peers.

Interactions with peers

In Chapter 5 I said that peers can provide an important way for people with PMLD to experience interactions in which they are equal partners. I also gave some examples of interactions in which both partners had PMLD. However, such interactions are inevitably constrained by the limited communication abilities of the people concerned. More inclusive settings in which people with PMLD get the opportunity to interact with peers without disabilities, or with fewer disabilities, might therefore seem to provide an ideal opportunity for them to participate in equal interactions and make social, communicative and cognitive progress. However, there is also a possibility that people with PMLD in integrated environments will experience unequal interactions with peers as well as with staff, since the probability is that peers, like staff, are more communicatively competent and they may therefore tend to dominate interactions.

Much of the research that has been done in inclusive settings has involved interventions designed to increase the participation of the students with disabilities. Often, in such interventions, social interaction is seen not so much as an end in itself but as a means to this end. Ways of increasing participation that specifically involve social interaction include peer-tutoring, buddy systems, 'special friends' projects and collaborative learning. In one of the few studies that did involve people with PMLD in interaction with their mainstream peers, Kennedy and Haring (1993) taught pupils with PMLD to request a change of activity using a microswitch, which effectively gave control to the pupil with PMLD (see next chapter). In another study, Putnam *et al.* (1989) compared two ways of introducing collaborative learning. They found that when students without disabilities were instructed in collaborative learning techniques and their use of these techniques was monitored, they interacted more with peers with moderate to severe disabilities. However, only initiations from the students without disabilities towards their disabled peers are reported. It is not clear therefore if students with disabilities responded more, or if they had more opportunities to initiate or lead interactions. In another study, of a life-science class which included two students with severe disabilities, Farlow reports that while on-task behaviour increased dramatically when a cooperative learning intervention was introduced, interactions, especially social interactions, decreased. Additionally a higher proportion of interactions involved teaching or helping. This may have meant that the interactions were dominated by the students without disabilities (Farlow 1994).

Thus interventions that focus on using interactions to increase participation in and mastery of the curriculum may potentially decrease the opportunities that people with PMLD have to take an equal share in interaction with their peers. Of course, the overall outcome of such interventions may be very positive in terms of student learning, but they also highlight the need to make specific provision for reciprocal social interaction between pupils with PMLD and their non-disabled peers.

Unfortunately, there are no studies of inclusive settings for people with PMLD that have focused primarily on the extent to which they experience a responsive environment from their peers. However, there are some studies of the different aspects of interaction which can throw light on the situation. Examining initiations and responses of two students with PMLD in integrated and segregated sessions, O'Connell (1994) found that both were engaged in so little peer interaction during the eight hours in which he observed that no conclusions could be drawn. Evidence from our own studies comparing integrated and segregated school settings (Ware *et al.* 1992) suggests (perhaps surprisingly) that children with SLDs *initiate* more during interactions with peers who also have learning difficulties. A similar finding is reported by LeRoy and Simpson (1996). However, they also report that students' initiations were more likely to receive a response in the integrated setting. A study by Beckman *et al.* (1993) throws further light on these findings by showing that toddlers with mild to moderate developmental disabilities initiated interactions more frequently with a familiar peer than with their mothers, even though, overall, they interacted for longer and in more complex ways with their mothers. Additionally, toddlers whose familiar playmate was closer to them in age initiated more than those with older playmates. Very importantly, mothers in this study were encouraged to select the playmate whom they felt their child interacted with most frequently; who could well have been the child's own choice of 'friend'. This research, together with that of Gleason (1990) detailed in Chapter 5, suggests that people with learning difficulties may be more likely to *initiate* interactions with other people who are operating at more or less the same developmental level. Thus at least one aspect of the responsive environment, the opportunity to take the lead in interactions, may require special attention in inclusive settings.

A detailed study by Ring (2000) of a boy with SLDs included full-time in a mainstream school may throw further light on the factors that influence responses from non-disabled peers to initiations from students with disabilities. She found that initiations from the disabled student (such as requests for the ball) during playground games were ignored. This contrasts with the findings of LeRoy and Simpson (above) and with those of Bang and Lamb, they found that over 95 per cent of initiations from students with disabilities were responded to positively by non-disabled peers. The explanation of this difference may lie in the type of activity being observed. Ring's observations are unusual in that they were of break-time activities. She indicates that the boy she observed did not understand the rules governing games such as football (such as being a member of a particular team), and it may well have been this that made his peers reluctant to include him, when at other times they acted protectively towards him.

Can anything be done to make inclusive environments more responsive?

One fairly clear finding from the research reviewed above seems to be that if inclusive settings are going to be responsive environments for people with PMLD then positive steps need to be taken to ensure that it happens. Structures need to be in place to enable both staff and peers to be responsive to people with PMLD. However, not all interventions have necessarily been positive with regard to all aspects of a responsive environment. For example, a number of studies report an increase in task-related interactions, which may diminish rather than increase the opportunities that people with PMLD have to take an equal share in interactions with their peers. Peers are frequently asked to act as 'peer-tutors' which may increase the likelihood that they will dominate the interaction. By contrast, a study by Hunt *et al.* (1992) concentrated on teaching students with moderate to severe intellectual disabilities to initiate and maintain conversations with non-disabled peers using a communication book. Peers were given relevant information to enable them to participate in interactions via the communication book, and regular opportunities were provided for conversations to take place. Both social and task-related interaction increased, and this was accompanied by a decrease in inappropriate ways of initiating interaction.

If you are coordinating a group working through this book together, identify any occasions on which the people with PMLD for whom you are responsible participate in activities with less-disabled peers. Review these activities with the help of the following questions:

- Are all the staff involved able to identify the meaning conveyed by different behaviours of the people with PMLD?
- Could they be helped to do so by participating in any of the exercises in Chapter 2?
- If this is not practical, could they be provided with simple written descriptions?
- Are peers able to understand the meaning conveyed by different behaviours of the people with PMLD?
- Could staff help them to understand through use of simple modelling techniques and commentary?

  E.g. 'See Michael's screwing up his eyes when you stroke him with the feather – he's trying to tell you he's really enjoying it. Why don't you ask him if he'd like "More feather?".'

  'Did you hear him say yes please with that sound he just made?'

- Could the activities be changed to provide more opportunities for cooperation and turn-taking?

Hunt *et al.*'s study is reported in some detail here, because copies of it are not easily obtainable, and (although the pupils Hunt and her colleagues worked with did not have PMLD) it appears to me to offer an exciting and practical way of helping people with PMLD and their non-disabled peers to engage in reciprocal social interactions.

Hunt *et al.* taught both the students with disabilities and their non-disabled peers to use 'turnabouts' (see Chapter 5) in order to 'promote equal participation and avoid domination by one partner'. In other words, both partners were taught to first respond to what their partner said and then to cue them to respond again, by a further question or comment. While people with PMLD might not be able to use a turnabout themselves, they might learn to wait for a response from their peer; while the peer could still be taught to deliberately use turnabouts.

In Hunt's study individual communication books, which consisted of coloured photos of favourite people and activities, were constructed for each student. Each picture was labelled with a short phrase which helped the partner to interpret the picture and provided suggestions for conversation. The students with disabilities were taught to pair spoken words with pointing to a relevant picture in the communication book. People with PMLD could be taught to point to their chosen picture, or simply hold it out to their non-disabled peer. Alternatively they might point and then sign or simply offer the book to their partner and then vocalise or indicate in some other way when the picture they want to 'talk about' was reached by a partner turning the pages.

Hunt first taught the students with disabilities to use the turnabouts with the communication book. Students were taught individually using a system of gradually faded prompts. Once they were able to use the system independently, their classmates were given a 30-minute lesson teaching them how to use the communication book with turnabouts to converse with the classmate with disabilities. Instruction included a demonstration and a role play activity in groups during which they were able to practise the relevant skills. After this, classroom staff initially provided reminders to peers at appropriate times (break, lunch etc.) that they could talk with peers with disabilities if they wished. Positive social interaction increased for all three students and inappropriate ways of initiating interaction decreased.

Similarly, a study by Cole (1986) used intensive instruction and modelling to teach non-disabled children to play with peers with severe and profound learning difficulties. He suggests that such interventions are more successful than peer-tutoring schemes at promoting reciprocal interactions with peers. Both Hunt's and Cole's studies address the twin issues of enabling peers to recognise the communications of people with PMLD and providing a context for interaction, and suggest possible ways forward if you are working in an inclusive setting.

Summary

The research reviewed in this section suggests that in order to create a responsive environment for people with PMLD in an inclusive setting, additional steps may be required to those outlined in the preceding chapters.

- The classroom needs to be organised to ensure that everyone gets an opportunity to participate by:
  - using small groups and 1:1 in preference to large groups;
  - using interactive toys which are fun for all those taking part;
  - organising cooperative activities.
- Mainstream peers may need:
  - information about the ways in which their peers with PMLD communicate;
  - help in giving peers with PMLD the opportunity to start interactions, and in responding appropriately to interaction attempts.
- People with PMLD may need teaching to initiate interactions appropriately.
- Staff may need training in facilitating interactions.

Moving on

If you have worked through the preceding chapters of this book and tried to apply the suggestions I have made in your everyday relationships with the people you work with, you may well already be aware of ways in which their communication skills are developing. In the Contingency-Sensitive Environments Project we found that becoming aware of the meaning of people's behaviour meant that staff responded more frequently to intentionally communicative behaviours. Our observations showed that when the pupils received these higher levels of response they communicated intentionally more often. For example, Dorothy originally experienced very few responses indeed to her attempts to communicate; staff responded to her on average only one in 12 times. When examination of Dorothy's behaviour made staff aware of the probable meanings of her behaviour, they dramatically increased the frequency with which they responded to her intentional communication, and Dorothy's intentional communications doubled. This suggests that simply being aware of how someone communicates is at least sometimes enough to change the pattern of interaction and begin a virtuous circle.

However, responses from those you work with to changes in your behaviour are not always so dramatic. Indeed it may sometimes be difficult to discern whether there has been any change at all, particularly in people's spontaneous initiations. So, if you have been experimenting with the strategies suggested in the previous chapters and trying to create a more responsive environment for the people you work with, you may well be wondering if your efforts are having any effect. Yet recognising such changes is important in adapting your own behaviour to facilitate further development.

One way in which such changes can be highlighted is by carrying out a reassessment of communication using the basic strategies described in Chapters 2 and 4. During the reassessment, behaviours identified previously as having communicative significance, being a response to an environmental event and so on, are examined in order to see if their meaning has changed or become clearer, or if they have become more frequent or consistent. Secondly, any new behaviours, or new uses of previous voluntary behaviours are identified. Finally, ways of facilitating further communicative development are considered.

For example, the original discussion about Carol (see Chapter 2) revealed the information summarised in Table 6.1. Changes in her behaviour during and after the project are shown in Table 6.2.

> If you are coordinating a group working through the book together, you will
> need to set aside some time (perhaps two periods of about half an hour) to
> look at the examples below and then hold a discussion about one of the
> pupils with whom you work.

At the start of the project, Carol was known to sometimes smile and make eye contact when an adult spoke to her; but no one knew why she sometimes responded in this way and sometimes didn't; indeed staff described her as moody. This description was reflected in our observations; Carol was responding to adults on average only one in three times. Examination of Carol's behaviour after the first period of staff training showed that she was responding more frequently (about one time in two, see Table 6.2). Clearly a further increase in the frequency with which Carol responded was desirable and, as the strategy that staff had been using (which was to remember to allow Carol plenty of time to respond, and to observe her closely, so that any small response she made was not missed) seemed to be working, it was continued. Ten months later, after a further period of staff training, Carol was responding four out of five times. This was obvious to the staff who worked with her who reported that she was less moody.

By the first reassessment everyone was also convinced that Carol's arm-lifting was intentionally communicative; however, it was still very infrequent, and this remained true at the second reassessment despite the fact that staff were managing to respond quite consistently to her. In other words, although the staff who worked with Carol were now consistently providing her with a highly responsive environment, only Carol's responses to initiations from others had changed significantly in response; her *initiations* remained very infrequent.

Table 6.1 Information recorded about Carol

Child: Carol			Date: 00/00/00
	Behaviour	Context	Frequency
INTENTIONAL COMMUNICATION	?Vocalisation	?To attract attention	Sometimes
	?Lifts her arm	?Trying to attract attention of nearby familiar adult	Infrequent
PURPOSEFUL BEHAVIOUR			
RESPONSES TO THE ENVIRONMENT	Sometimes moves head	When objects appear in her line of vision	Sometimes
	?Vocalisation	?Hearing two familiar adults talking to each other	
	?Lifts her arm	When familiar adult is working nearby	Infrequent
RESPONSES TO INITIATIONS FROM OTHERS	Smiles and makes eye contact	When an adult speaks to her	Sometimes
VOLUNTARY BEHAVIOUR	?Vocalisation	Various	

How could Carol's communicative development be further facilitated? In particular, how could she be encouraged to initiate interactions more frequently?

One possibility is to capitalise on the success that staff have already had in getting Carol to respond to their initiations, for example by developing a turn-taking game. Such a game might involve Carol and a member of staff alternately putting items away in a box, alternately pressing a switch (see next chapter), as well as the more obvious alternate vocalising or use of a musical instrument. Once Carol

Table 6.2 Information recorded about Carol following a reassessment of her communication during and after the project

Child: Carol			Date: 00/00/00
	Behaviour	Context	Frequency
INTENTIONAL COMMUNICATION	?Vocalisation *Lifts her arm	?To attract attention *Trying to attract attention of nearby familiar adult	Sometimes Infrequent
PURPOSEFUL BEHAVIOUR			
RESPONSES TO THE ENVIRONMENT	Sometimes moves head ?Vocalisation	When objects appear in her line of vision ?Hearing two familiar adults talking to each other	Sometimes
RESPONSES TO INITIATIONS FROM OTHERS	Smiles and makes eye contact	When an adult speaks to her	*About half the time **Usually
VOLUNTARY BEHAVIOUR	?Vocalisation	Various	

*changes noted at first reassessment
** changes noted at second reassessment

had learned the game and was consistently taking her turn, the staff member working with her might omit to take an expected turn and wait for a reaction from Carol, which could then be treated as an initiation requesting them to take their turn. The technique used by Richard with Tommy in Chapter 5 could also be adopted, with situations being set up where the control of the interaction could easily pass to Carol; or routines could be used (see below).

Alternatively, examination of Carol's responses to environmental events (turning her head when something comes into her visual field, and vocalising) suggests that staff might decide to respond to these as if they are intentional communications, as well as continuing to respond to her arm-lifting. Thirdly, staff could make special efforts to ensure that Carol had something to communicate about (see below). Finally ICT might be used to magnify Carol's communication attempts (see next chapter).

Exercise

Reassess one of the people for whom you carried out an assessment in Chapter 2, concentrating initially on those behaviours that you originally decided to respond to as if they were intentional communications. Have any of them become more frequent? Do you now think that any of them are intentionally communicative? How do you know? For example, with a behaviour that you think is intended to attract attention, does it stop when you give the individual attention, and restart if you leave, as Tanya's did? (See Chapter 5.) On the basis of this information, decide what strategies to adopt in order to help the individual concerned develop their communication skills further.

Using routines

Throughout this book I have drawn parallels between the ways in which you and other adults interact, and ways in which you interact with people who have profound and multiple learning difficulties. These parallels have been drawn, not simply in order to make the ideas I am trying to get across easy to follow, but because I believe that there is strong evidence that the basic structure of human interaction is the same regardless of whether a professor of philosophy is talking to a theologian about the existence of God, two children are excitedly discussing their proposed trip to Alton Towers, you are having an intimate conversation with a close friend, a teenager is helping her mother choose a new dress, a five-year-old is helping his big sister clear up, a toddler is sharing a picture book with her aunt or a father is talking nonsense with his baby daughter. However, despite the common framework, there are important differences between these conversations in the extent to which the different partners take responsibility for the structure and continuance of the interaction.

In the first four examples it is likely that the two partners take equal responsibility, while in the last three one partner takes more responsibility than the other, ranging from the father who is more or less completely responsible for seeing that the conversation continues, to the big sister who can probably rely on her little brother to take about an equal share.

Within the framework of turn-taking, caregivers interacting with infants without disabilities seem naturally to adjust the way in which they interact as the infant develops, and this adjustment assists the infant's further development, as they are encouraged to take a greater share of the responsibility for the interaction. This adjustment is much harder with someone with profound and multiple learning difficulties for all the reasons mentioned in Chapter 1 (difficulties in picking up the rhythm of their behaviours, difficulties in 'reading' behaviour and expressions in order to know how they feel, conflicts between the expectations engendered by their appearance and the way they behave and expectations brought about by the 'label' that has been attached to them) and because, as I have already mentioned, the changes in behaviour that signal development may be so slow as to be almost imperceptible.

Routines

If someone, like Carol, responds to initiations only inconsistently, it is easy to repeatedly use any pattern of interaction that we know is likely to get a response. For example, if a particular individual almost always responds with smiles and chuckles to a game involving being bounced on someone's knee, and only rarely responds to other attempts at starting an interaction, we are likely to repeat the game again and again because it 'works'. There are some very positive features to familiar routines such as these: they provide a framework of turn-taking within which development is possible, and caregivers use them, not just with very young infants, but also with toddlers whose communication skills are developing. For example, the routine involved in playing a body-part game can develop from a simple one question, one answer situation (Where's your nose?) through a series of questions and answers (Where's your nose/eyes/ears?) and then showing parts on different bodies (Where's teddy's nose?) to a situation where the infant may point to a body-part and the caregiver supply the name, and finally to the infant naming the body-part concerned (Snow *et al.* 1982) as the child involved develops more sophisticated communication skills. There are simpler games than this such as 'Round and round the garden' which are also capable of development as the infant becomes familiar with them. In such games, the more competent communicative partner provides a number of slots for the other partner's responses; the numerous repetitions of the game (they may be played 20 or more times a day by caregivers and young infants) enables both partners to take their turns successfully.

Penny and Jill, two of the teachers in the project schools, had developed routines for use with small groups of their pupils. Penny's game consisted of tapping on and looking in a box of assorted objects to select one. The children with whom Penny played this game were at varying stages of communicative development, and the game had a number of stages, as shown below.

Penny's tapping game: basic format

Penny:	*Timmy*, your turn to look in the box.
Timmy:	(hands on box)
Penny:	(taps and sings) Tap, tap, tap, *Timmy*, *Timmy*, what's inside?
Penny:	(Turns box so opening is on top)
Timmy:	(hands in box)
Penny:	Oh, oh... *Timmy*, look what's coming out!
	R-e-a-d-y
	It's a...

Although all that is initially expected as a response from the child in this game is to look, or respond in some other way as the object emerges from the box at the end, it was capable of a good deal of development and elaboration. Penny introduced pauses after 'look what's coming out' and 'ready' to allow any child who was ready for this step to look and anticipate the toy emerging. Eventually, the child could tap the box themselves, or initiate the game by reaching for the box, both of which we observed Timmy do.

In fact, although I have described this game for one child, Penny played it with a group, adjusting the way in which she played as she moved from child to child.

The routine began with Penny sitting in front of a semi-circle of children with the box, and singing her tapping song. Although this aspect of the routine was at a very sophisticated level compared with the current level of communication skills possessed by some of the children in the group, the regular repetition gives an opportunity for anticipation to develop, and individuals to respond to seeing the box in ways that can be treated as initiations. For example, one child might increase their level of activity or vocalise more, and Penny could then respond by saying 'That's right, we're going to look in the box. Do you want first go?'

However, the children with whom we watched Penny play this game (Katie, Ben, Tracey and Darren) had not yet developed this level of anticipation, so Penny selected one child (Katie) to start. The song was sung, and Katie was helped to pull out the Christmas decoration from the box. For Katie, Penny hopes at this stage merely to momentarily break her self-absorption and achieve eye contact. As she becomes used to the routine, and in response to Penny's skill in selecting objects that attract her, Katie may reach out to grab one of them, and this can become the start of a turn-taking routine with Penny.

As part of the routine of the game, Penny now shows the object (Katie's choice) to the other members of the group. This provides further opportunities for anticipation, initiations, and mini turn-taking routines with individuals. For example, on one occasion Tracey showed great interest in the decoration and even moved one hand towards Penny, providing further opportunities for turn-taking.

With Darren, Penny tries to introduce a more sophisticated level of turn-taking by placing the object on his head, and this provides an opportunity for Ben's eye-tracking of the object (probably a response to the environment – see Chapter 2) to be treated as an initiation by Penny responding as if he has asked for a turn.

When it comes to Tracey's turn, after Penny has sung the song with the box held very near to her, Tracey (somewhat uncertainly) hits the box once – she is beginning to learn the routine and take her part in it successfully.

Jill's game, which was a good morning song, incorporating pauses for the child to respond, was also played with a group. In both cases the fact that the game was played with a group, while it meant that each individual received fewer repetitions themselves, had the advantage of helping them to anticipate that their turn was coming by hearing the game played with others, and provided additional opportunities for initiations.

Routines such as Penny's tapping game have enormous potential for development, but it is also possible for routines to become 'fossilised' or sterile. The game may be repeated in an identical format time after time, with no space allowed for elaboration or the partner to take a more active part in it. Being aware of the ways in which caregivers and infants develop their routines as the infant becomes more competent can help in ensuring that the routines you use with the people with whom you work have the potential for development.

Exercise

Identify routines that you use on a regular basis with more than one individual, or a routine that you have used with one person over a period of time. In what ways does a particular routine change when you use it with different individuals? Has the routine you have used for some time changed over time? Is it possible to put these changes in order of complexity? Are any of your routines unchanging (and potentially fossilised)? Identify places where you could introduce developments, by writing out the routine in the format given (p.97) above for Penny's tapping game, and examining ways you could enable the other person more opportunities to respond or anticipate the next part of the routine (for example by leaving pauses).

One of the problems of trying to capitalise on the advantages of routines with older people with PMLD is that those that come immediately to mind are likely to be games played by caregivers with young infants, which are not age-appropriate with older people. However, this does not have to be the case; routines can be part of reading a book together, and could even be introduced into tasks such as laying the table. Familiar tasks such as this in which both language and actions are highly predictable can provide the opportunity for gradually increasing participation and control in a similar way to a game routine.

Additionally, in our more intimate relationships, we often indulge in very familiar game-like routines even as adults. A couple may have routines in their private times together consisting of highly predictable turns. The group of young people walking across newly mown grass and attempting to stuff it down each other's necks may well be repeating a routine. The family of parents and teenagers playing beach cricket quite possibly indulge in stylised rituals which have developed out of routines introduced when the children were much younger.

The groups of adult friends, as well as those of young teenagers, playing on the giant inflatables in the swimming pool near where I used to live, were often engaging in highly predictable routines. One person would climb onto the swaying inflatable and as the inflatable rocked (or was rocked by the other person) would fall off again into the water.

In these situations, the routines seem, as they are, a natural part of human friendship, and their predictability and repetitiveness is a valued part of the overall interaction. What may make such routines seem strange with adults with profound learning difficulties is not that they are not age-appropriate, but that, instead of developing 'naturally', they may need to be deliberately introduced and developed. However, there may also be times when you inadvertently impede routines that the people with whom you work are developing for themselves (see the example from Gleason's work in Chapter 5). Becoming more aware of the meaning of people's behaviour also needs to be extended to their behaviour with peers, and particularly in making an extended assessment of someone's social interaction abilities, as Gleason suggests, observation of what they do with peers when you are not intervening can make a crucial contribution.

Other ways of facilitating the development of communication skills

Other aspects of the environment also need attention if people are to develop more sophisticated communication and social skills. One of the problems for people with PMLD is that their lives may often be so impoverished that they have little to communicate about. By saying that their lives are impoverished what I mean is that they may be expected to use the same materials or visit the same places day in and day out, year in and year out.

Having something to talk about

Although, as I have said in earlier chapters, the content of a conversation is not always important – we may interact with our friends for the sheer pleasure of interacting; we also communicate enjoyable and novel experiences that have stimulated us to those who are important to us and, when we share such experiences, we converse about them. On a shopping trip we notice some unusual garment, 'Look at that coat! Can you imagine being seen in that?' We visit a beautiful garden with a friend, and discovering a delicate flower hiding in a corner, we point it out to them: 'Look, at this, isn't that pink fantastic.' I am frequently laughed at by friends and family for the cry of 'Look, primroses!' or 'violets!' which I'm likely to come out with whenever we come across these flowers on a walk or a journey. But my pleasure at the unexpected appearance of splashes of colour on a motorway verge or in a hedgerow is an occasion for communication. If on foot, we may bend to examine the flowers more closely: 'Don't they smell gorgeous' or 'Look, this one's paler than all the others.' Even the small talk at a party suggests that it's easier to get a conversation going if we have something to talk about.

A friend of mine, who teaches a PMLD class, tells me that when he provides novel materials for his students, they behave in much the same way, examining the items and showing them to others. The novelty of the objects and the opportunity to interact freely with them gives them something to communicate about, and they display their most sophisticated communication skills in this situation (Park, personal communication). The opportunity to handle things freely rather than just being shown them is an essential part of this experience because of the early developmental level at which people with PMLD are likely to be operating. Novel experiences of this type can be created in a number of fairly simple ways which do not involve using childish materials. To give just two examples: in a school situation, the artefacts that might be used as part of a geography or history session, if robust enough to be handled, could be put out for people to examine freely. The variety of things that are to be made into a collage can be put out for people to examine before use. An additional way of increasing Carol's initiations (see above) might well be to offer her some new materials or experiences. A sound-sensitive mat, soundbeam or resonance board might well elicit environmental responses from Carol, which could then be responded to as initiations. If you regularly take a group of people with PMLD on the same outing, always calling at McDonald's for coke and chips, you might arrange to turn into a different nearby restaurant for, say, strawberries and cream.

Extending routines asking for 'more'

In Chapter 5 I gave examples of how different people with PMLD indicated that they did or didn't want a particular game to be continued or repeated. Another way in which people can be helped to develop their communication skills is by establishing a consistent 'more' signal. For example, Emma tended to vocalise in response to sensations she enjoyed such as being fanned. Ann successfully developed this into a 'more' signal by interspersing her actions with pauses during which she asked 'More fan, Emma?' and waited for Emma's vocalisation before starting the action again. Ann then introduced some sensations she knew Emma did not like (such as a foil Christmas decoration and a whistle). Emma tended to respond to these sensations by looking down or away. Again, Ann interspersed her actions with pauses in which she asked 'More Emma?' only repeating the action if Emma vocalised. When I watched Ann working with Emma, Emma was able to use a vocalisation consistently to ask for more and looking down or away to say 'no more' (See Figures 6.1a–e.).

Figure 6.1a Ann fans Emma and **b** Emma vocalises to ask for 'more'

Figure 6.1c Ann blows the whistle and **d** and **e** Emma indicates 'no more' by her facial expression and by turning away

Staffing

One of the things that we noticed in the research project was that some children responded especially to particular members of staff. Perhaps the most striking example of this was Jonathan's response to Flo, which was mentioned in Chapter 2. Jonathan did not communicate intentionally, yet he appeared to recognise Flo's voice and respond to it as he did not respond to the voices of other adults. Discussion with Flo revealed that she and Jonathan had known each other for many years. Not only did Jonathan recognise Flo, but (not surprisingly) she was particularly skilled in interpreting his behaviour. This meant that Flo was potentially a key person in helping Jonathan to develop more sophisticated communication skills, not simply by responding when Jonathan vocalised at the sound of her voice (as suggested in Chapter 2) but also in other ways which capitalised on the special rapport between them.

In a busy environment involving a number of staff and pupils, ensuring that there were opportunities for Flo and Jonathan to enjoy turn-taking games together (for example) might well require special planning. However, given the difficulties in interpreting the behaviour of people with PMLD and their problems in recognising unfamiliar individuals, the recognition of a particular rapport between an individual with PMLD and a member of staff provides an important opportunity for mutually enjoyable interactions, and thus for the development of communication.

However, providing opportunities for people with PMLD to spend time with members of staff they get on with particularly well, is not the only way in which the organisation of staff can facilitate their development. Both staff turnover and movement of people with PMLD between groups or classes can mean that the staff who interact most regularly with an individual with PMLD change frequently. Additionally, both the sheer numbers of staff involved and the use of volunteers can mean that large numbers of unfamiliar people interact with a person with PMLD. For people who are operating at a very early level, it may be appropriate to limit the numbers of staff and volunteers who interact with them, as familiarity may well assist communication. For everyone, while meeting new people is important, organising staff so that there is always someone familiar around can help in ensuring that an individual's behaviour is understood and responded to. This may be particularly important in inclusive settings.

Additionally, even simple routines such as playing a body-parts game are carried out in different ways by different people, and different individuals will also have their own preferred routines. Join in a game of rounders with a number of families on the beach, and the first thing that has to be negotiated is exactly what the rules are. Often in environments for people with PMLD we try to make roles which are fillable by a number of different staff. Of course, this is necessary for smooth organisation and has many advantages; but at the level of individual interactions, people are not interchangeable, and the different ways in which we do things are important parts of our personality. When someone with PMLD is learning a new routine, therefore, it is probably best if it is carried out by the same staff member each time; as the routine becomes familiar, the natural variations in the way it is used by different staff members can provide new learning opportunities.

Cognitive progress

The evidence that was discussed in Chapter 1 suggests that the strategies that promote the development of communication will also facilitate cognitive progress. So recognising communicative development and moving on in this area is likely also to encourage cognitive development. However, it can be just as hard, if not harder, to recognise progress in cognitive development as in communication. One of the problems is possibly the way in which we are currently encouraged to think about progress, which tends to devalue the achievements of people with PMLD; and can also have a knock-on effect on staff. Because this issue is vitally important to the question of how a responsive environment can be kept going on a long-term basis, it will be discussed in more detail in Chapter 8.

Summary

Being aware of the ways in which an individual communicates can mean that we respond more frequently to them and that this, in turn, encourages them to communicate more often.

- It is sometimes very difficult to notice the progress that people with PMLD are making; reassessment and knowledge of likely developments from their current behaviour can help us to become aware of changes in their behaviour.
- The general framework of communication remains the same regardless of who is participating in the interaction, but the balance of responsibility between the partners alters according to their communication skills.
- Routines that increase the likelihood of someone with PMLD participating in the interaction can provide a useful framework for the development of communication but we need to be alert to the danger of them becoming 'fossilised'.
- Organisation of staff and provision of novelty can also help in developing communication skills.

CHAPTER 7

Using Technology to Extend the Responsive Environment

One of the most noticeable changes that has occurred in the half dozen or so years since the first edition of this book is the increase in the number of publications about the use of information and communications technology (ICT) with people with PMLD (e.g. Bozic and Murdoch 1996; Pagliano 1999; Taylor 1998). There is also now a huge range of IT equipment available from sophisticated multisensory environments to simple switch-operated toys and Big Macks. Used appropriately such IT equipment has great potential for enhancing the responsiveness of the environment for people with PMLD, and thus their quality of life. However, in comparison with the potential, the benefits so far to people with PMLD from switch technology seem comparatively slim.

In this chapter I examine some of the ways in which IT can be used to contribute to the creation of a responsive environment, and discuss how to make the best of the opportunities that IT provides. I also look at some of the potential pitfalls in using IT and suggest how they can be avoided. Consequently this chapter focuses on three main uses of ICT:

- as a way of magnifying the communication attempts of people with PMLD
- as a support for the curriculum – a teaching tool
- as an aid to monitoring performance and assessing progress.

Of course, ICT is also a curriculum subject in its own right, but this chapter is not about teaching ICT, but about how ICT can be used as a tool, both by staff and by people with PMLD themselves.

Because the research project on which the first edition of this book was based did not include the use of ICT, and there are very few examples of people using ICT to enhance the responsiveness of the environment in a practical way, the suggestions in this chapter are more tentative than those in the rest of the book.

As a way of magnifying communication attempts

In Chapter 2 I looked at the problem of people with PMLD communicating in ways that are extremely easy to miss in a busy environment such as a classroom or day centre. In that chapter I described Carol, whose most sophisticated form of communication was to slowly raise her arm. The staff who worked with Carol worked hard to ensure they didn't miss her very occasional attempts to attract attention in this way, and they were successful. However, technology could potentially provide a more fail-safe alternative to the strategies that they adopted, by turning Carol's arm-lifting into a more noticeable signal. For example, a tilt switch on Carol's arm might operate an audible signal to alert staff. (And if this signal was one of Carol's own recorded vocalisations, Carol might eventually 'get the message' and vocalise herself as well as lifting her arm.) What such a use of technology is doing is magnifying or translating a small signal to make it more noticeable. Of course, instead of using one of Carol's own vocalisations we might choose to use a speech output device of some sort to translate Carol's arm-lifting into a particular message such as 'Hi, it's Carol: please speak to me.'

The difference between *magnifying* the signal (as in the use of a non-specific vocalisation or a buzzer) and *translating* it (as in the case of the message 'please speak to me') is an important one. If we simply magnify the signal we are leaving its meaning open to interpretation by whoever happens to respond on any particular occasion. One member of staff might respond by offering to move Carol so that she could see what was going on better, another might speak to her, while another might engage in a brief chat or offer her a change of activity. If we translate the signal by arranging for Carol's arm-lifting to operate a specific message, it's likely that everyone will respond in a broadly similar way, for example by saying 'hello' and engaging in social chat.

In order to translate a signal such as Carol's arm-lifting we have to make an inference as to its meaning. Often, as I suggested in Chapter 2, this is an entirely appropriate thing to do, and consistently interpreting a particular behaviour to mean 'please speak to me' or 'I want to see what's going on' can help an individual to develop intentional communication. In Carol's case, the fact that she began to raise her arm more often (see Chapter 6) and that staff became convinced that it was an intentional behaviour, suggests that their interpretation that she wanted attention was correct.

A recent review by Lancioni, O'Reilly and Basili (2001) summarises a number of attempts to translate the idiosyncratic communication of people with PMLD into speech. The rationale for this approach is that speech is the most effective form of communication and so, if the communications of people with PMLD can be translated into speech, they are more likely to receive responses. Potentially, therefore, the use of speech output systems can increase the responsiveness of the environment for people with PMLD.

One example of a successful attempt to do this is given in a study by Schepis and Reid (1995). They worked with a young woman called Megan whose communication attempts consisted of non-speech vocalisations and gestures. These were often very difficult to interpret. Megan was trained to use a VOCA (Voice Output Communication Aid) on which she could ask for an item by pressing its photograph. Pressing a photograph resulted in a spoken request for the item. The advantages of this system over a picture board, which could be presented to Megan to enable her to make choices, were that:

- It enabled her to ask for an item at any time when she had access to the VOCA.
- It increased the extent to which she was involved in responsive interactions with staff.

In fact, according to Schepis and Reid, during sessions when Megan had the VOCA staff interactions with her were more than doubled (compared with non-VOCA sessions) and most of these interactions began as responses to requests from Megan. A follow-up later showed that Megan was still experiencing an enhanced level of responsiveness to her requests. As Schepis and Reid themselves point out, this is one of the few documented accounts to use a VOCA with someone with a profound level of learning difficulty. This may have something to do with the intensity of teaching required to enable individuals with PMLD form the initial association between the items and their photographs, which is made clear in a subsequent paper by Schepis, Reid and Behrman (1996).

However, the use of such a system to magnify and clarify communication attempts appears to have considerable potential once an individual is able to make choices between items, as Megan clearly was.

Magnifying communication attempts at the pre-intentional level

Almost all the people in the studies mentioned by Lancioni *et al.* (2001) could already communicate intentionally, although their intended meanings (as in Megan's case) may have been unclear and easily missed. Many people with PMLD have not reached this level of communication. For example, in Chapters 2 and 6 I mentioned the fact that several of the pupils in the project schools tended to vocalise when they heard an adult speaking to another child. Studies of typically developing infants suggest that they too find the sound of an adult talking to another child appealing, and are probably simply 'joining in' in the way they would if the adult was talking to them. If then an individual with PMLD responds to the sound of a familiar voice by moving their hands excitedly rather than vocalising, it may well not be appropriate to translate this to a specific meaning, such as 'Hello'. It might be more appropriate to arrange for a switch to translate the hand movements into non-specific vocalisations or even a light display, thus ensuring that the signal was not missed and the individual could receive a response, without attributing an over-specific and possibly incorrect meaning.

Additionally, if an individual has only very limited communication and uses one signal to mean a variety of different things, providing one specific translation for a signal can be especially problematic. For example Luke, who was one of the pupils involved in the Contingency-Sensitive Environments Project, used to communicate by banging with one hand on his helmet. However, this didn't always seem to have the same meaning. Depending on the context this behaviour might most appropriately have been interpreted: 'Yes, I'd love a chat' (in response to a member of staff who had spoken to him); 'Hurry up with that drink!' (when the process of giving him a drink was interrupted); or 'Go away!' This helmet-banging behaviour of Luke's did not need magnifying; like most potentially self-injurious behaviours it never failed to get a response, and it is not clear that giving it one particular meaning would have helped Luke to communicate more effectively. On the other hand, carefully assessing Luke's communication behaviours to see if he had any less salient means of communicating, and magnifying this so that it achieved the same level of response as his helmet-banging, might in time have reduced the extent to which he resorted to this particular way of communicating.

One study that did include people who did not yet communicate intentionally was that conducted by Kennedy and Haring (1993). Four people with PMLD, none of whom were able to communicate intentionally, were involved in this study. Physical prompts were used to teach them to press a microswitch linked to a tape recorder to request a change of activity when they ceased to be engaged with the activity on offer. When they had learned to do this, mainstream peers were introduced; and the individuals with PMLD were able to ask their peer for a new activity by pressing the switch. The microswitch enabled the individuals with PMLD to control changes of activity during these sessions, thus providing them with a more responsive environment.

These examples suggest that one important decision that you need to make about individuals who are operating at the pre-intentional level is whether simply to magnify their communication attempts or to attempt to translate them as well. One way you might decide which is most appropriate for a particular individual is to review the information you collected about individuals' communication abilities in Chapter 2. Where a signal that someone gives is generally agreed by those who know them best to be intentional and to mean something specific (even if that's only 'I want some attention') but could easily be missed or misinterpreted by someone who knows the individual concerned less well, then a translation may be appropriate, and an appropriate switch might be used for this purpose, as in the example of Carol (above). A translation may also be appropriate for some responses to the environment, for instance if someone often bangs on their tray when they hear someone come into the room, a switch could be used to translate this to 'Hello, please come and speak to me.'

Pitfalls of using a single switch–single message set-up

However, it can be tempting to use a switch (especially the Big Mack) to give an over-specific message. Contrast, for example, the two scenarios below:

Tina (a staff member) enters the room.

Matthew bangs on his tray.

Tina goes over and speaks to him: 'Hello, Matthew, nice to see you.'

Matthew bangs on his tray again.

Tina: 'Sorry, Matthew, I can't really stop for much of a chat now, I've just come to collect something for Alan.'

Matthew bangs again.

Tina: 'No, sorry I really can't stop.' She moves away and calls out 'Cheerio then Matthew, see you again soon.'

Matthew bangs again and Tina leaves the room.

Tina (a staff member) enters the room.

Matthew bangs on his tray and this activates a switch which says 'Hello, it's Matthew, I'd like a chat.'

Tina goes over and speaks to him: 'Hello Matthew, nice to see you.'

Matthew activates the switch again, which again says 'Hello, it's Matthew, I'd like a chat.'

It's clear from this second scenario that the attempt to translate Matthew's banging as a greeting when he also uses it as a conversational turn has reduced Tina's flexibility to interpret it in a way that enables her to continue the interaction. An alternative might be for her to remove the switch when she goes over to speak to Matthew, replacing it as she leaves. This example may seem far-fetched, but the version with the switch is in fact adapted from an actual incident. I was visiting a school on one occasion where a number of the children had Big Macks or similar devices which were programmed with a 'hello' message. They were prompted to greet me using their switches but then reactivated the switch when I went to have a conversation with them.

Similarly I was told of two of the pupils setting up a conversation across the classroom by turn-taking with their Big Mack switches. Although the switches undoubtedly allowed the two to engage in an interaction from a distance, the interaction was limited by the fact that the switches repeatedly delivered the same verbal message. A more complex interaction, with more opportunity for control to pass back and forth between the two participants, might have resulted if the first initiation and response had been treated as a mutual request to play together and the two pupils concerned had been moved into a position where they could touch each other or share a toy. For example, they could have been introduced to a computer programme or switch-operated toy which required each to operate their switch for the next action to occur.

Of course, a 'hello' message might work well for someone who is able to communicate intentionally but unable to vocalise loudly or clearly enough to attract attention. One example of the use of such a system is reported by Schweigert (1989). He worked with a seven-year-old girl called Shannon who was operating at about a three-month level. Shannon first received social reinforcement (stroking and verbal praise) for operating a switch. When she had learned this the switch was used to operate a tape loop which requested attention. Schweigert and Rowlands (1992) point out that getting attention is only the first step in developing the skills to use high-tech communication aids such as those used by multiply disabled individuals who do not have learning difficulties. Where staff agree that a person uses the same signal to mean different things on different occasions, or have great difficulty agreeing the meaning of a particular signal but still think that it could easily be missed or not seen as a communication attempt by those who know the person concerned less well, it's probably better to use a non-specific magnification, at least in the first instance.

> If you are coordinating a group working through this book together, arrange a time when you can meet to discuss whether any of the people you work with would benefit from having their communication attempts magnified or translated. Remember that if the translation involves deliberately activating a switch using a specific movement, a highly structured teaching programme may be required to teach the individual to use the switch before they can use it to communicate (see the example of Megan above).

Planning ahead

While being able to magnify or translate the pre-intentional communication attempts of people with PMLD is important, it is also very important to realise the limitations of doing so using a single switch that conveys a single message. The second scenario with Matthew given above is only one example of these limitations. It's also important to plan ahead, so that if a person is given a single switch to magnify their attempts to attract attention, you know how you are going to try and develop this to give them a variety of meanings.

Although a number of researchers have successfully taught people with profound disabilities to use individual switches and there are also some studies where two or more switches have been used to enable the individual to make discriminations or choices, there is little that is easily accessible to help teachers and care staff plan the development of communication using ICT.

However, Schweigert and Rowlands (1992) have developed an instructional sequence which uses microtechnology to support the development of communication and social interaction for children with multiple disabilities in an attempt to bridge the gap between the development of social contingency-awareness (as in the example of Shannon) and the use of sophisticated communication aids. The first four stages of this sequence are:

1. attracting attention;
2. showing interest in an object or activity;
3. making choices;
4. making choices using symbols.

Schweigert and Rowlands stress that microtechnology is only a means to an end within this system, being used only to ameliorate physical disabilities and enhance the responsiveness of the environment. Accordingly switches are only used at any stage in the sequence if the child's natural communicative behaviours are not clear enough to gain reliable responses. Eleven children were involved in the three-year project that Schweigert and Rowlands describe, and they give detailed results for three who made progress to stage three or four, of whom at least one had been classified as having profound learning difficulties at the start of the project. This child, Jordan, was initially taught to use a switch to gain a musical reinforcement. This was subsequently paired with a social reinforcer. By the time the project finished, Jordan was making choices by tactually scanning 3D symbols, and then reaching to touch the one he wanted. Schweigert and Rowlands point out that they were not successful in teaching all 11 children using these methods. However, their work does suggest a way in which the use of switches to attract attention can be developed into more sophisticated communication behaviours.

As a support for the curriculum

Another use of ICT which is perhaps particular to schools is as a tool through which aspects of the curriculum can be delivered. For mainstream pupils computers are used for a wide range of curriculum support activities, for example drill and practice and gathering information. In these support activities an important criterion for the use of ICT is either that it represents the most effective way to teach a particular thing to a particular pupil or that it provides an additional avenue for exploration and practice. So, in relation to pupils with PMLD if a critical aspect of the curriculum is teaching pupils that they can get responses to what they do, then ICT may provide a vehicle for teaching this. Of course, ICT may be used with pupils with PMLD for many other purposes, for example teaching discrimination, tracking or visual perception; but in this chapter I am only concerned with the use of ICT to support the creation of a responsive environment. The criteria for selecting ICT as the medium of choice remain the same as in mainstream, that it provides a particularly effective way of teaching for a particular individual, and/or offers opportunities for practice.

Teaching contingency awareness

As I mentioned in Chapter 1, babies normally get experience of a responsive environment in two ways: from the people around them and from the material environment. In the normal course of events, social contingencies come first. It is other people who give babies their first experiences of getting responses to what they do. For example, when a baby vocalises, it is likely to get a response from any nearby adult. Then, at about three months old, they begin to learn that objects around them can also respond to them. As I discussed in Chapter 1, children with multiple disabilities find both these types of contingency harder to learn than typically developing children because they tend to give less clear signals, and are able to interact with the material environment in only very limited ways. If then the use of ICT can improve the chances of people with PMLD receiving consistent feedback to their actions, it can be a valuable tool in the provision of a responsive environment.

Over the past 20 years or so, there have been a number of studies in which both typically developing babies and people with multiple disabilities (mainly but not exclusively children) have been taught to operate single switches in order to get a particular response, such as music, a light display or the operation of a toy. In such studies learning is usually judged by an increase in the rate of switch-pressing when the contingency is in force.

A careful look at these studies suggests that they are generally quite unlike what teachers and care staff would usually do when trying to teach someone to use a switch. For a start, the switch is not normally demonstrated nor its use prompted either verbally or physically, rather it is set up in such a way as to enable the child to come into contact with it by accident. Secondly, most of the studies are experimental in nature and have been conducted by researchers who either take the individuals concerned to a laboratory setting or provide additional personnel and other resources to the school or other facility to conduct the experiment *in situ*. Where studies have been conducted by practitioners, details of procedures are often unavailable. Thus few studies are concerned with the issue of how the individual who has acquired contingency-awareness through the use of ICT can be helped to develop a more general sense of being able to affect their environment. Finally, particularly in the earlier studies it is often not possible to tell whether the individuals concerned had a profound level of learning difficulty in addition to multiple physical and sensory disabilities. Despite these limitations, this experimental work has been successful in teaching the participants (at least some of whom undoubtedly did have PMLD) at least the early stages of contingency-awareness through the application of ICT.

For example, Watson, Hayes and Vietze (1982) report the results of a series of experiments with an eight-month-old girl with severe/profound learning difficulties. This child successfully learned to operate a pressure-sensitive pillow with three distinct movements to obtain different stimuli, and she also showed enjoyment of the sessions by smiling, although she had not previously been observed to smile. Additionally, she appears to have learned a more complex contingency in which one stimulus (operated by leg-kicks) was only available after a light and buzzer had been switched on by an arm movement. Her parents and foster parents were both delighted with her apparent enjoyment of the experimental sessions. O'Brien, Glenn and Cunningham (1994) conducted sessions over the period of a week with seven children with severe/profound learning difficulties using leg or arm movements to activate a reinforcer via a beam switch. The four children who showed definite evidence of learning, all learned in the first session in which they were presented with contingent reinforcement, and also smiled more during these sessions. Dunst, Cushing and Vance (1985) conducted sessions with six boys with profound learning difficulties over periods ranging from a day to a week. Four of their six participants acquired contingency awareness. Dunst *et al.* comment that there are impacts not only on the child, who appears to enjoy the learning situation, but on the parents who see their child behaving in ways that appear competent and are likely to be more responsive to the child as a consequence. Thus in terms of enhancing the responsiveness of the environment, Dunst suggests that teaching contingency-awareness using ICT may have indirect as well as direct effects.

Where teaching is successful, it seems that the participants in the experiment often appear to enjoy the sessions, smiling, laughing and operating the switch for extended periods. By contrast, when the contingency is removed (either as part of the experimental design or by accident), they frequently show distress. Furthermore, under the learning conditions described, participants often learn remarkably quickly, increasing their rate of switch-pressing within the first one or two contingent sessions. Work with secondary-aged pupils with PMLD briefly reported by Taylor (1998) seems to support these findings within a classroom environment.

Although most studies rely on positioning the switch so that it will be operated accidentally, rather than using prompts, whether or not prompting is used, positioning of the switch so that it can be consistently contacted and give absolutely consistent responses is crucial. However, using switches to provide contingent responses to people with PMLD is not as simple and straightforward as it might sound. As Lancioni, O'Reilly and Basili (2001) point out, there are a number of obstacles to the successful use of switches to teach (or extend) contingency-awareness. Where an individual has PMLD, the choice of switch, the response with which it is to be operated, and positioning are likely to be crucial to successful teaching, and may require the involvement of physio and occupational therapists (Lancioni *et al.* 2001). Schweigert and Rowlands (1992) similarly point out that it may sometimes take months to find a suitable switch set-up for a particular individual, and even then the difficulties of operation may mean that it is not really useable within the individual's normal everyday environment. Work by Higgins (personal communication) in which prompts were used to teach a girl called Sonya with PMLD to use a switch suggests that the considerable time taken in teaching was exacerbated by the difficulty of positioning the switch satisfactorily. Sonya, like the participants in the studies in the literature, demonstrated great pleasure in her achievements, eventually learning to use a switch to operate 'Switchit' software.

In some work we have recently begun in Ireland, we have found that issues to do with the selection and positioning of the switch, the ease with which the equipment can be set up and its reliability play a major role in the feasibility of using such methods in ordinary classrooms in the normal course of the day and as an integral part of the curriculum (Ware, Thorpe and Mehigan, in preparation). Yet if the potential of ICT for enhancing the responsiveness of the environment is to be realised, then it needs to become an ordinary part of settings for people with PMLD.

Multisensory rooms

Many people with PMLD now have access to a multisensory room with a range of devices which may or may not be switch-operated. If such an environment is to be used to support the curriculum and enhance learning, careful planning is required so that the aims of the session are clear for particular individuals. The most important decision is whether the multisensory room is going to operate simply as a fun environment to explore, or as a responsive environment. If it is to be a responsive environment, which individuals within a group will have the opportunity to control the stimulation? Will it be possible to avoid the situation where stimulation that was under a particular individual's control now seems to be operating randomly, because control has passed to a peer?

As an aid to monitoring performance and assessing progress

A further issue raised by Schweigert and Rowlands (1992) in relation to using ICT to support the learning of contingency-awareness is that, unless data is collected to show whether or not switch-pressing increases when there is an interesting consequence available, it can be difficult to decide whether or not learning has taken place. One of the ways in which ICT seems currently to be very underutilised is for keeping records of this sort. While research studies employ computer technology to count switch-presses and monitor activity levels, most equipment available in schools and other settings consists simply of switches attached to leisure items, functional devices or brief recorded messages. This means that staff have to count switch-presses as well as prompt the person who is learning. Consequently it is also much more difficult to see if there is a pattern to switch-pressing, for example if the rate of switch-pressing begins to decline part way through a session. ICT, even at the level of operating a single switch, can also be very valuable for demonstrating that someone is responding consistently and, as Dunst (1985) points out, this may change the view that you and others have of them; from someone who is able to do very little and needs constant input, to someone who is able to exercise some control over their own environment and enjoys doing so.

Summary

ICT seems to have great potential for enhancing the responsiveness of the environment for people with PMLD, both by providing a way of communicating and as a support to the curriculum, especially for teaching contingency-awareness.

At the time of writing, this potential remains largely unrealised but it seems most likely that ICT will be utilised successfully for these purposes where:

- Carefully planning as to the further development of switch use takes place before switches are introduced.
- Non-specific communication attempts are magnified to make them more noticeable and thus more likely to attract a response.
- Communication attempts that can have a clear meaning attached to them are translated to ensure a consistent response.
- Use of switches to teach contingency-awareness is supported by assessments to ensure that switches are appropriately selected and positioned.
- The potential of the computer to record data automatically is utilised, and staff are given training in interpreting and using this data.

CHAPTER 8

Keeping the Responsive Environment Going

The last six chapters of this book have been concerned with how you can adjust the environment you provide for the people with PMLD with whom you work in order to make it more responsive. With the exception of the last chapter, I have concentrated almost exclusively on how this can be done through interaction. Of course, as Watson *et al.* (1982) and Glenn and O'Brien (1994) have suggested, for some people ICT may provide a bridge to satisfying social interaction by enabling them to develop contingency-awareness, and by helping others to see that they enjoy getting responses to what they do. It may also have an important role in widening opportunities for people with PMLD to experience a responsive environment, but I believe that social interaction is of primary importance. Therefore, in this concluding chapter I return to the fundamental issue of how you can create and maintain an environment in which people with PMLD have increased opportunities to get responses to their actions, give responses to the actions of others and take the lead in interaction. The rationale for this approach is that by providing such opportunities, you will encourage interactions in which both partners participate more or less equally, even though it may well be that you, as the more competent partner, will be taking the lion's share of the responsibility for making this happen. I think interactions of this sort are valuable because they facilitate communicative, social and cognitive development, enhance self-esteem and contribute to making your own role satisfying and enjoyable.

However, particularly if you are coordinating a group working through this book together, you may be wondering 'What next?' and 'How do I make sure that I/we carry on interacting in positive ways?'

To some extent, a responsive environment may maintain itself. If, as you have adjusted the ways in which you interact, the people with whom you work have become more responsive and are developing communication skills, you will be getting some positive feedback about the impact of your efforts, and this will have made the job of providing them with a responsive environment somewhat easier.

But that may not be enough. After all, at least part of the reason why people with PMLD often do not automatically experience a responsive environment is that they do not provide sufficient feedback to keep positive interactions going. When you are in a hurry, as you are likely to be quite often, it is hard to remember to keep giving opportunities to respond to someone who never seems to take them. Yet a consistently responsive environment is particularly important for people who do not immediately respond to it, who may include those who have experienced years of living in an environment in which they have not been expected to participate. These people may need prolonged experience of responsive interactions if they are to learn that participating is worthwhile. In these circumstances you need to make special efforts to ensure that the responsive environment continues. In the remainder of this chapter I explore three strategies that can contribute to maintaining a responsive environment: increasing feedback, considering the activities you provide and the way in which you provide them, and thinking about what we mean by progress.

Increasing feedback

If your interactions with those you work with do not provide you with sufficient feedback to ensure that you continue to interact in positive ways, the obvious solution is somehow to get feedback by some other means. One important part of the Contingency-Sensitive Environments Project was that it provided the staff who took part with additional positive feedback. Both in group sessions and in individual meetings with staff, we were able to use our observations to demonstrate that their efforts to provide a responsive environment were being successful.

Jean and Tommy: drinks

For example, on one occasion at drinks time Tommy (who was sitting alone at a table) continued to pick up his mug and attempt to drink from it after it was empty.

> As she approaches him, Jean calls out, 'Tommy, would you like some more? Because that's empty.'
>
> Tommy puts down his mug (which falls over) and turns towards her.
>
> Jean rights the mug and looks closely at Tommy (who turns to her again). She asks, 'Would you like more to drink?' She then tries to wipe Tommy's mouth, but he pushes her away. Jean says, 'I know you don't like it.' She then moves slightly so she is looking directly into Tommy's face and repeats slightly more loudly, 'Would you like more to drink?'
>
> Tommy again picks up his empty mug and attempts to drink. Jean says, 'Would you like more? Let's get the orange.' She reaches for the jug of squash and places it on the table. Tommy puts down his mug.

Jean again asks, 'Do you want more, Tommy?' He reaches for the jug and looks at it.

All the time Jean is observing Tommy closely.

Jean says, 'Good boy, hold the juice.' But as she puts her hand on the jug to help him pour, he removes his hand. Jean says, 'Hold it' and places his hand back on the jug handle saying, 'and pour it into your cup.' Tommy keeps his hand on the jug handle and continues to look as the squash is poured into his cup.

As Tommy lifts his mug to drink, Jean removes the jug. Then she adjusts Tommy's table, commenting to herself in a low voice as she does so, and leaves Tommy to drink.

Discussion with Jean would start by asking her how she feels she is getting on with putting the responsive environment into practice. Feedback might then go something like this: 'I think you are responding more to the children's initiations. I really liked that time I saw you giving Tommy his drink the other day, I thought it was brilliant, you assuming that drinking from the empty cup like that meant he wanted more. You gave him lots of time to respond and he was really responding, looking at you and the jug, *and* keeping his hand on the handle and that was really good for him.'

Getting feedback of this type is much easier if you are part of a group than if you are an individual working through this book alone. However, there are some strategies for ensuring that you receive positive feedback that are available to you even if you are working alone, or in an unsympathetic environment. The most obvious is to arrange to video some of your interactions (as suggested in earlier chapters) and then pick out examples that you feel particularly positively about (for instance, of occasions when you gave the other person the opportunity to respond). Although it is likely to feel strange, try and be specific with yourself about why you see the aspects of the interaction that you have selected as positive. For example, if Linda was reviewing her own interaction with Mary, which was described in Chapter 4, she might feel especially positive about the repeated opportunities she gave Mary to respond, when Mary seemed completely unresponsive. If videoing is not possible, you can still give yourself positive feedback, by 'rerunning' each interaction of the day in your mind and highlighting one positive aspect.

However, it is well worthwhile trying to obtain some video, especially of those people who seem particularly unresponsive, even if you can only borrow a camera occasionally, since it may well enable you to spot responses that are normally very difficult to see. Knowing that someone is responding to your efforts to create a responsive environment is very positive feedback indeed. Additionally, once having spotted a subtle response on video, you can be on the alert for it in the future. When Mary and I looked at video of Damien (see Chapter 2), we came to the conclusion that he responded more positively to her than to me; but his responses were so subtle that they could easily be missed. Mary found this very encouraging, and it increased her confidence in herself as a teacher; she was being more successful than she realised. Furthermore, as these responses were very small it would be possible to think about a strategy for magnifying them to make sure that they were not missed in future (see Chapter 7).

Exercise

Set aside a few minutes at some time during the day, and use them to review your last two or three interactions with those with whom you work. You may find it helpful to write out a list of those you interacted with, in order, and then beside each name write down one positive thing about the interaction. You may wish to do this with regard to one aspect of the responsive environment at a time. For instance, you might look simply for occasions when you gave the other person the opportunity to respond to you. You might draw up a simple table like the one below. This table is not intended as a record of interactions, just as a way of helping you think about them.

Table 8.1 Information about interactions

People with whom interactions took place	Date/Time: 14.12.02/9.25
Micky	Having asked Micky if he was ready for work I waited to see if he would acknowledge me at all. Eventually he made eye contact.
Diksha	I asked Diksha to get her coat and waited to see if she would walk over to the coat pegs before prompting her again.

As you look for positive factors you will inevitably notice the not so good things as well. Try to see these in a positive light; noticing them gives you the opportunity to further develop your interactional skills.

If you are coordinating a group working through this book together, try and identify with each group member a convenient time when they can spend just a few minutes reviewing their last few interactions, for example by making available an extra five minutes before coffee break or lunch break each day for different members of staff.

Whether you are working through this book by yourself or as a member of a group, it is important that these exercises are repeated at regular intervals if you are going to ensure that the responsive environment is maintained. Time constraints and other training priorities will almost inevitably mean that you can only carry out detailed video or other observations once every several months, but in the intervals in between, you can carry out the exercise above on an individual basis with occasional opportunities to share positive feedback, if you are working as a group.

A responsive environment for staff

Another way to use video for positive monitoring, but on an individual basis, is to pair members of staff and provide the opportunity for them to video each other interacting with a particular individual, and then watch the video together to give positive feedback. If at all possible, let the pairs select themselves and make sure that you have emphasised the importance of positive feedback.

If you are coordinating a group working through this book together and you have access to video equipment, arrange to video one individual pupil/client at intervals over a week or so. These video sessions do not have to be very long, five to ten minutes is ample. You may well be able to set up the video where it can 'see' the individual without the need for an operator. Unless the video needs to be in close-up in order for you to see an individual's responses, you are likely to find it more useful to have video that shows the surroundings as well, as this gives you a better chance to work out if an individual's behaviours are triggered by environmental events. View the video yourself and select positive examples for use as feedback at a meeting of your group. This technique is particularly useful with individuals who have previously been identified by the group as receiving little positive interaction. Try and use a balance of two types of positive example; ones that demonstrate that responsive interactions are getting results, and ones that demonstrate members of staff being persistent even when they don't appear to be getting results.

You will need to have some time available for selecting the examples you wish to show, and to be particularly careful to avoid inadvertently showing parts of the tape where people are interacting in less positive ways.

If you do not have video, it may be that you are in a position to arrange for different members of staff to observe individual pupils/clients at intervals. For example, you might ask different members of staff to observe one particular individual at different times during the week noting occasions, for example, when they were given opportunities to take the lead in interaction. As with video, individual observations do not need to be very long – ten minutes is ample. When these observations are discussed, you will need to start by reminding people that feedback is to be positive. So, the observers could start by highlighting the times when they had seen a colleague giving an opportunity to take the lead in interaction. Only then would the group discuss how they could apply the techniques described in the earlier chapters of this book to give the individual concerned more opportunities to take the lead. To end the discussion you would re-emphasise the positive examples and the range of strategies available to the group for giving the individual concerned opportunities to take the lead.

You could also ask members of the group to share positive examples of interaction that they have happened to observe in the course of the day.

Less formally, you can encourage members of the group to comment positively on each other's interactions as they go about their work.

If you are working alone, but have a line manager who is responsible for monitoring your work, you might consider asking them to give you feedback on specific aspects of your interactions with the people you are responsible for. For example, you could highlight the fact that you were trying to give people the chance to respond during routine activities such as moving rooms, and ask for positive feedback.

These ways of providing positive feedback to yourself and other members of the staff group may seem rather contrived or even cold. But noticing and appreciating the ways in which other members of your team interact with people with PMLD and listening to their ideas and concerns is actually a way of showing them that, like the people with PMLD with whom you work, they are valued and respected as persons. Apart from the philosophical and moral arguments for this position, there is plenty of evidence to suggest that both being treated with esteem and consideration and being ignored and devalued rub off on those with whom we come into contact.

Planning activities

It has been my experience that where the main aim of an activity is the production of a particular thing, whether a Christmas cake, Mother's Day card, wooden tray or whatever, the interactions that take place between staff and people with PMLD tend to offer little opportunity for participation by the person with PMLD. In Chapter 3 I mentioned that in the research project we found a similar lack of opportunities for participation in activities, such as individual work, where a specific response is demanded of the person with PMLD. Perhaps the problem with both these types of activities is with the way in which they are frequently focused: focusing on either a particular product or a particular response may mean that you become blinkered to other aspects of the interaction. If this is the case, then attention to the planning and organisation of these sorts of activities should help.

Whether you plan on paper, or simply by thinking about possible activities and ways of carrying them out, it is important to include a stage where you consider what responses you might expect to get from those people with the most severe difficulties. One individual may smile if they like the feel of something, and another withdraw their hand or turn away when they don't. One stage in the production of a Mother's Day card could be sticking tissue paper onto glued card. If while this operation is taking place someone responds by withdrawing their hand from the tissue, rather than pressing it onto the glue, having planned for the possibility of this response, you will be in a position to acknowledge its meaning. For instance, you might comment, and then offer alternative materials. Obviously this would involve planning in order to have alternative materials (such as felt pieces or cotton wool) readily available. Over time, this response might be developed into a signal which the individual could use to request a change of materials or activity in a similar way to that described in the study by Kennedy and Haring (see Chapter 7).

If a product is involved, it is useful to think about what parts of the process are likely to be possible for each individual. For example, in her session making bread with Mary in Chapter 4, Linda concentrates on the process of kneading the dough. Although Mary has very profound learning difficulties, she does sometimes move her hands, and so it is possible that she will press the dough; and even if she doesn't, she may react to (and enjoy) its unaccustomed feel, and thus participate in the process.

So, I am not suggesting that people with PMLD should not be participating in activities such as carpentry, cookery, gardening and so on. Indeed the novelty of some of the materials used in these activities may encourage them to communicate. Rather I am suggesting that activities such as these can be done in a way that is consistent with providing a highly responsive environment; by incorporating consideration at the planning stage of the ways in which the individuals involved are likely to respond.

One consequence for the staff in the project classes of providing a more responsive environment for their pupils was that they found activities taking longer than they had previously, and thus they were able to get through fewer things in the course of a day. This probably happened as the result of staff slowing down their interactions to give the pupils more time to participate. So another important feature of maintaining a responsive environment is to build some flexibility into the timing of activities. This may be very difficult, especially where each individual has a complex timetable of activities designed to meet their individual needs, but it is worth aiming for. There is little point in rushing from work experience to hydrotherapy, if you do not get the opportunity to participate in either.

> If you are coordinating a group working through this book together, arrange to collect information, in advance of individuals' reviews, about whether the organisation of their day allows sufficient time for them to participate fully in the various activities of which it is made up.

Progress

Caregivers of young infants get feedback partly from the baby's developing skills. The baby is interesting to be with, partly because with each passing day they are able to do more; the range of sounds they make increases, there is more variety in the way they respond to different people and so on.

In the previous chapters of this book, especially Chapter 2, I have emphasised the importance of increasing your own sensitivity to the meaning of people's behaviour for the development of interaction and communication; and if you have examined the behaviour of the people you work with in the ways I have suggested then you have probably already become aware, not only of the meaning of some of their behaviours, but also of the ways in which their behaviour has changed over time. In working through Chapter 6 you may have been alerted to progress that you hadn't previously noticed. In saying this, I am not suggesting that you should have noticed this progress; rather that progress can be very difficult to spot. Being able to discover progress where previously you were unable to see it is important for maintaining a responsive environment, because being able to see that what you are doing is having a positive impact on the lives of the people you work with provides the feedback and encouragement we all need to keep us going.

Recognising progress has three important elements. I have already discussed two of these in relation to the development of communication; first, an increased sensitivity to changes in behaviour and second, knowledge of the normal course of development. The third factor that can contribute to recognising progress is to examine the way we think about progress.

Increasing sensitivity to changes in behaviour

As I have suggested in earlier chapters, video can be an important tool in increasing your sensitivity to subtle responses. In the same way it can alert you to small changes in behaviour that may indicate progress. Some schools already use video records as part of a pupil's portfolio. However, the type of video records that are likely to be most useful for demonstrating progress, especially for people with the most profound disabilities, are likely to be taken specifically for that purpose and accompanied by carefully structured notes.

For example, video of Paul, one of the pupils who took part in the Contingency-Sensitive Environments Project, revealed that he showed anticipation when given repeated turns on the slide (an activity he particularly enjoyed). Video collected in this and other situations that Paul was known to enjoy could enable his progress to be monitored. Video collected as the class was going to the school hall where the slide activity took place could be examined for evidence that Paul anticipated his first turn. Repeated turns at other enjoyable activities could also be set up and videoed for evidence of anticipation. Progress might be shown by Paul showing anticipation in the appropriate setting before his first turn.

Video of Damien taken when Mary came into the room and spoke to him might reveal if he recognised her at some level before she touched him, again giving evidence of progress. As with Paul, careful structuring of the situation to allow Damien the chance to recognise Mary and careful note-keeping would be needed.

Thinking more flexibly about progress

In Chapter 6 I mentioned that the way we usually think about progress, which is in terms of progress towards predefined objectives, may not be particularly helpful in recognising the progress of people with PMLD. When we talk about progress, we often do so in terms that imply that there is some absolute standard against which it can be judged. But just thinking about the everyday use of the word 'progress' suggests that this is far from true. For example, the recent announcement of road building and widening schemes in England is viewed by some people as progress, but by others as close to madness. Similarly, the protests over the Newbury bypass (which were going on as I prepared the first edition of this book) illustrated graphically the differences in view within one comparatively small community about what constitutes progress. The differing priorities of different groups and individuals lead them to have very different views as to what constitutes progress in all sorts of areas.

In the research project, in addition to observing the interactions of staff and pupils and offering training to the staff, we also talked to them about (among other things) their idea of progress as it related to children with PMLD.

Several of the staff were very clear that many of those with no experience of people with PMLD would come to the conclusion that they made no progress; but they were also clear that this was due to taking a rather narrow view of progress; and in a school context, stressing academic attainment, exam success or even self-help skills. As I have already suggested, it is not only educational views of progress (or success) that are problematic for people with PMLD, but the general way in which our society thinks about it.

I am not suggesting that there is some new definition of progress which will solve the problem with regard to people with PMLD. Rather, in the light of our discussions with the staff from the project classes, I have concluded that the most useful way to think about this issue is to be as flexible as possible.

At the very earliest developmental level, for example, we might, as one of the teachers suggested to us, see as progress someone being awake for more of the day, or not crying all the time they are away from home, settling more quickly after a holiday, or as reacting differently when they spend time away from their familiar surroundings, or taking their turn in a way that invites you to have another go, as well as in all the more usual ways.

This is not to say that the acquisition of new skills and of conventional ways of communicating is not important; there is no doubt that being able to communicate in ways anyone can understand is important; rather that even if we cannot discern any progress in these areas, there may well be other important ways in which progress is happening.

On this view, it is progress if someone who has been unhappy and upset is now happier and more settled. It is certainly progress if you are now able to tell when someone is saying that they prefer being helped by one person than another, even if that may be mainly because you have improved at interpreting the meaning of different facial expressions.

Summary

In summary: the responsive environment may not maintain itself; but it can be maintained by:

- Ensuring that staff receive positive feedback through positive monitoring.
- Positive monitoring can be carried out by observing yourself and others with or without the help of video.
- Planning activities to include responses that you know are possible for the individuals concerned and developing a wider view of what constitutes progress can also help to maintain a responsive environment.

Conclusion

In this book I have tried to show that a responsive environment is important for people with PMLD, as it is for all people, because it facilitates the development of social awareness, communication and cognition, and makes life more enjoyable for staff. And above all because it demonstrates that people with PMLD are respected and valued as individuals. I have also tried to demonstrate that such an environment can be created and maintained with the meagre resources for staff development and training usually available in settings for people with PMLD.

References

Anderson, C. J. and Sawin, D. (1983) Enhancing responsiveness in mother-infant interaction. *Infant Behaviour and Development* 6, 3–18.

Aspin P. N. (1982) Towards the concept of a human being as a basis of a philosophy of Special Education. *Education Review* 34, 11–23.

Bang, M. and Lamb, P. (1996) The impact of inclusion of students with challenging needs. Paper presented at the Annual Conference of the Association for Persons with Severe Handicaps, New Orleans LA, November.

Barber, M. and Goldbart, J. (1998) Accounting for learning and failure to learn in people with profound and multiple learning disabilities. In Lacey, P. and Ouvry, C. (eds) *People with Profound and Multiple Learning Disabilites: A Collaborative Approach to Meeting Complex Needs.* London: David Fulton Publishers.

Barrera, M. E., Rosenbaum, P. L. and Cunningham, C. E. (1986) Early home intervention with low-birth-weight infants and their parents. *Child Development* 57, 20–33.

Barrera, M., Rosenbaum, P. and Cunningham, C. (1987) Corrected and uncorrected Bayley scores: Longitudinal developmental patterns in low and high birthweight preterm infants. *Infant Behavior and Development* 10(3), 33–46.

Barrera, M. and Vella, D. (1987) Disabled and non-disabled infants' interactions with their mothers. *American Journal of Occupational Therapy* 41(3), 16–72.

Barrera, M., Watson, L. and Adelstein, A. (1987) Development of Down's syndrome infants with and without heart defects and changes in their caretaking environment, *Child: Care, Health and Development* 3(2), 87–100.

Beckman P., Leiber, J. and Strong, B. (1993) Influence of social partner on interactions of toddlers with disabilities: Comparisons of interactions with mothers and familiar playmates. *American Journal on Mental Retardation* 98(3), 37–89.

Bozic, N. and Murdoch, H. (1996) *Learning through Interaction: Technology and Children with Multiple Disabilities* London: David Fulton Publishers.

Bray, A. (1988) Social Interaction at Home of Young Children with Down's Syndrome. Paper presented at the 8th IASSMD Congress Dublin, August 1988.

Breiner, J. and Forehand, R. (1982) Mother-child interactions: A comparison of a clinic-referred developmentally delayed group and two non-delayed groups. *Applied Research in Mental Retardation* 3, 17–83.

Campbell, P., Leib, S., Vollman, J. and Gibson, M. (1989) Interaction pattern and developmental outcome of infants with severe asphyxia: A longitudinal study of the first years of life. *Topics in Early Childhood Special Education* 9(1) 48–71.

Cole, D. A. (1986) Facilitating play in children's peer relationships: Are we having fun yet? *American Educational Research Journal* 23(2), 20–115.

Cole, D. A. and Meyer, L. (1991) Social integration and severe disabilities: A longitudinal analysis of child outcomes. *Journal of Special Education* 25(3), 340–51.

Coupe O'Kane, J. and Goldbart, J. (eds) (1998) *Communication Before Speech* (2nd edition). London: David Fulton Publishers.

Cunningham, C. E., Reuler, E., Blackwell, J. and Deck, J. (1981) Behavioural and linguistic development in the interactions of normal and retarded children with their mothers. *Child Development* 52, 62–70.

Dichtelmiller, M. L. (1995) A longitudinal investigation of mother-infant interaction and its relationship to cognitive development: Differences between very low birth weight and full-term infants. *Dissertation Abstracts International Section A: Humanities and Social Science* 55(8-A), 22–71.

Downing, J. and Seigel-Causey, E. (1988) Enhancing the non-symbolic communicative behavior of children with multiple impairments. *Language, Speech and Hearing Services in Schools* 19, 33–48.

Dunst, C. J. (1985) Communicative competence and deficits: effects on early social interactions. In McDonald, E. T. and Gallagher, D. L. (eds) *Facilitating Social-Emotional Development in Multiply Handicapped Children.* Philadelphia: Home of the Merciful Saviour.

Dunst, C., Cushing, P. and Vance, S. (1985) Response-contingent learning in profoundly handicapped infants: A social systems perspective. *Analysis and Intervention in Developmental Disabilities* 5(1–2), 33–47.

Durand V. M. (1990) *Severe Behavior Problems: A Functional Communication Training Approach.* New York: Guilford Press.

Farlow, L. (1994) Co-operative learning to facilitate the inclusion of students with moderate to severe mental retardation in secondary subject-area classes. Paper presented at the 118th Annual Meeting of the American Association on Mental Retardation. Boston MA: May 31–June 4.

Favell, J., Realon, R., and Sutton, K. (1996) Measuring and increasing the happiness of people with profound mental retardation and physical handicaps. *Behavioral Interventions* 11(1), 47–58.

Felce, D. (1998) The determinants of staff and resident activity in residential services for people with severe intellectual disability: Moving beyond size, building design, location and number of staff. *Journal of Intellectual and Developmental Disability* 23(2), 10–19.

Field, T. (1983) High risk infants have 'less fun' during early interactions. *Topics in Early Childhood Special Education* 3(1), 77–87.

Fraiberg, S. (1977) *Insights from the Blind: Comparative Studies of Blind and Sighted Infants.* New York: Basic Books.

Garrad, K. (1986) Mothers' questions to delayed and non-delayed children. *Journal of Childhood Communication Disorders* 9(2), 95–106.

Gleason, J. J. (1990) Meaning of play: Interpreting patterns of behavior of persons with severe developmental disabilities. *Anthropology and Education Quarterly* 21, 59–77.

Glenn, S. and O'Brien, Y. (1994) Microcomputers: Do they have a part to play in the education of children with PMLDs? In Ware, J. (ed.) *Educating Children with Profound and Multiple Learning Difficulties.* London: David Fulton Publishers.

Goldbart, J. (1980) Play Context and Language in the Special Classroom. Seminar Paper. Manchester, Hester Adrian Research Centre.

Goldbart, J. (1994) Opening the communication curriculum to students with PMLDs. In Ware, J. (ed.) *Educating Children with Profound and Multiple Learning Difficulties.* London: David Fulton Publishers.

Goldberg, S. (1977) Social competence in infancy: A model of parent-infant interaction, *Merrill Palmer Quarterly* 23, 16–77.

Golden, J. and Reese, M. (1996) Focus on communication: Improving interaction between staff and residents who have severe or profound mental retardation. *Research in Developmental Disabilities* 17(5), 36–82.

Gomes-Pedro, J., Patricício, M., Carvalho, A., Goldschmidt, T., Torgal-Garcia, F. and Monteiro, M. (1995) Early intervention with Portuguese mothers: A 2-year follow-up, *Developmental and Behavioral Pediatrics* 16(1), 218.

Hanzlik, J. R. (1990) Non-verbal interaction patterns of mothers and their infants with cerebral palsy. *Education and Training in Mental Retardation* 25(4), 33–43.

Hanzlik, J. R. and Stevenson, M. B. (1986) Interaction of mothers with their infants who are mentally retarded, retarded with cerebral palsy, or nonretarded. *American Journal of Mental Deficiency* 90, 51–320.

Harris J., Cook, M. and Upton, G. (1996) *Pupils with Severe Learning Disabilities Who Present Challenging Behaviour: A Whole School Approach to Assessment and Intervention.* Kidderminster: BILD.

Hauser-Cram, P. (1993) Paper presented at the 60th Meeting of the Society of Research in Child Development, New Orleans, March 27.

Hewett, D. and Nind, M. (eds) (1998) *Interaction in Action.* London: David Fulton Publishers.

Hile, M. and Walbran, B. (1991) Observing staff:resident interactions: What staff do, what residents receive. *Mental Retardation* 29, 35–41.

Houghton, J., Bronicki, G. and Guess, D. (1987) Opportunities to express preferences and make choices among students with severe disabilities in classroom settings. *Journal of the Association for Persons with Severe Handicaps* 12, 1827.

Hunt, P., Alwell, M. and Goetz, L. (1992) The regular class as a communication support group. Report to the Office of Special Education and Rehabilitative Services, Washington DC.

Jones, E., Perry, J., Lowe, K., Felce, D., Toogood, S., Dunstan, F., Allen, D. and Pagler, J. (1999) Opportunity and the promotion of activity among adults with severe intellectual disability living in community residences: The impact of training staff in active support. *Journal of Intellectual Disability Research* 43(3), 164–78.

Julian, G. (2002) Curriculum and provision for pupils with profound and multiple learning difficulties in England, Wales and Ireland: A comparative study. Unpublished PhD thesis School of Social Sciences, University of Wales, Cardiff.

Kaye, K. and Charney, R. (1981) How mothers maintain dialogue with two year olds. In Olson, D. (ed.) *Social Foundations of Language and Thought.* New York and London: Norton Press.

Kennedy, C. and Haring T. (1993) Teaching choice making during social interactions to students with profound multiple disabilities. *Journal of Applied Behavior Analysis* 26, 63–76.

Kuder, J. and Bryen, D. (1993) Conversational topics of staff members and institutionalised individuals with mental retardation. *Mental Retardation* 31, 148–53.

Lancioni, G., O'Reilly, M. and Basili, G. (2001) Use of microswitches and speech output systems with people with severe/profound intellectual disabilities: A literature review, *Research in Developmental Disabilities* 22(1), 21–40.

Landesman-Dwyer, S. and Sackett, G. (1978) Behavioral changes in nonambulatory profoundly mentally retarded individuals. In Meyers, C. E. (ed.) *Quality of Life in Severely and Profoundly Retarded People: Research Foundations for Improvement.* Washington DC: American Association on Mental Deficiency.

Letourneau, N. (1999) The effect of improved parent-infant interaction on infant development: Pilot study. *Dissertation – Abstracts International: Section-B: The Sciences and Engineering* 59(12-B), 6504.

Lewis, M. and Coates, D. L. (1980) Mother-infant interactions and cognitive development in twelve-week-old infants. *Infant Behavior and Development* 3, 95–105.

McCollum, J. A. (1984) Social interaction between parents and babies: Validation of an intervention model. *Child: Care, Health and Development* 10, 301–15.

MacDonald, J. D. and Gillette, Y. (1984) Conversation engineering: A pragmatic approach to early social competence. *Seminars in Speech and Language* 5(3), 171–83.

Mahoney, G. and Robenalt, K. (1986) A comparison of conversational patterns between mothers and their Down syndrome and normal infants. *Journal of the Division for Early Childhood* 10(2), 17–80.

Mahoney, G. and Powell, A. (1988) Modifying parent-child interaction: enhancing the development of handicapped children. *The Journal of Special Education* 22(1), 82–96.

Mencap (1999) *On a Wing and a Prayer.* London: Mencap.

Minde, K., Whitelaw, A., Brown, J. and Fitzhardinge, P. (1983) Effect of neonatal complications in premature infants on early parent-infant interactions. *Developmental Medicine and Child Neurology* 25(6), 76–7.

Murray, L. and Trevarthen, C. (1986) The infant's role in mother-infant communication. *Journal of Child Language* 13, 15–29.

Nind, M. and Hewett, D. (1994) *Access to Communication.* London: David Fulton Publishers.

Nind, M., Kellett, M. and Hopkins, V. (2001) Teachers' talk styles: Communicating with learners with severe and complex learning difficulties. *Child Language Teaching and Therapy* 17(2), 143–59.

O'Brien, Y (1991) Reactions to response-contingent stimulation in non-handicapped infants and multiply learning disabled infants and children. Unpublished PhD thesis, University of Central Lancashire.

O'Brien, Y., Glenn, S. and Cunningham, C. (1994) Contingency awareness in infants and children with severe and profound learning disabilities. *International Journal of Disability, Development and Education* 41(3), 231–43.

O'Connell, R. (1994) Proving integration works: How effective is the integration of students with PMLDs into the mainstream of an SLD school in increasing their opportunities for interaction? In Ware, J. (ed.) *Educating Children with Profound and Multiple Learning Difficulties.* London: David Fulton Publishers.

Pagliano, P. (1999) *Multisensory Environments.* London: David Fulton Publishers.

Paton, X. and Stirling, E. (1974) Frequency and type of dyadic nurse-patient verbal interactions in a mental subnormality hospital. *International Journal of Nursing Studies* 11, 135–45.

Putnam, J., Rynders, J., Johnson, R. and Johnson, D. (1989) Collaborative skill instruction for promoting positive interactions between mentally handicapped and nonhandicapped children. *Exceptional Children* 55(6), 550–57.

QCA (2001) *Planning, Teaching and Assessing the Curriculum for Pupils with Learning Difficulties.* Series of 15 Booklets. London: QCA.

Realon, R., Bligen, R., La Force, A., Helsel, W. and Goldman, V. (2002) The effects of the positive environment programme (PEP) on the behaviors of adults with profound cognitive and physical disabilities. *Behavioral Interventions* 17, 1–13.

Ring, E. (2000) Unpublished MEd Thesis Special Education Department, St Patrick's College, Dublin.

RNIB (1995) *One of the Family: 1. First Sight. 2. Going my Way. 3. Making Contact. 4. That's What It's All About!* London: RNIB.

Schaffer, H. R. and Liddell, C. (1984) Adult-child interaction under dyadic and polyadic conditions. *British Journal of Developmental Psychology* 2, 33–42.

Schepis, M. and Reid, D. (1995) Effects of a voice output communication aid on interactions between support personnel and an individual with multiple disabilities. *Journal of Applied Behavioral Analysis* 28, 73–7.

Schepis, M., Reid, D. and Behrman, M. (1996) Acquisition and functional use of voice output communication by persons with profound multiple disabilities. *Behavior Modification* 20(4), 451–68.

Schweigert, P. (1989) Use of microswitch technology to facilitate social contingency awareness as a basis for early communication skills. *Augmentative and Alternative Communication* 5, 192–8.

Schweigert, P. and Rowlands, C. (1992) Early communication and microtechnology: Instructional sequence and case studies of children with severe multiple disabilities. *Augmentative and Alternative Communication* 8, 273–86.

Scoville, R. (1984) Development of the intention to communicate: The eye of the beholder. In Feagens, L., Garvey, C. and Golinkoff, I. R. (eds) *The Origins and Growth of Communication.* New Jersey: Ablex Publishing Corporation.

Seys, D., Duker, P., Salemink, W. and Franken-Wijnhoven, J. (1998) Resident behaviors and characteristics as determinants of quality of residential care: An observation study. *Research in Developmental Disabilities* 19(3), 261–73.

Shonkoff, J. P. *et al.* (1992) Development and infants with disabilities and their families: implications for theory and service delivery. *Monographs of the Society for Research in Child Development* 57(6), 1–153.

Snow, C. (1984) Therapy as social interaction: Analyzing the context for language remediation. *Topics in Language Disorders* 4(4), 72–85.

Snow, C. E., Dubber, C. and de Blauw, A. (1982) Routines in mother-child interaction. In Feagans, L. and Farran, D. C. (eds) *The Language of Children Reared in Poverty: Implications for evaluation and intervention.* New York: Academic Press.

Spiker, D., Boyce, G. C. and Boyce, L. K. (2002) Parent-child interactions when young children have disabilities. In Glidden, L. M. (ed.) *International Review of Research in Mental Retardation.* San Diego CA: Academic Press.

Taylor, J. (1998) In Lacey, P. and Ouvry, C. (eds) *People with Profound and Multiple Learning Disabilities: A Collaborative Approach to Meeting Complex Needs.* London: David Fulton Publishers.

Terdal, L. E., Jackson, R. H. and Garner, A. M. (1976) Mother–child interactions: A comparison between normal and developmentally delayed groups. In Mash, E. J., Hamerlynck, L. A. and Handy, L. C. (eds) *Behaviour Modification and Families.* New York: Brunner/Mazel.

Veit, S. W., Allen, G. J. and Chinsky, J. M. (1976) Interpersonal interactions between institutionalised retarded children and their attendants. *American Journal of Mental Deficiency* 80, 535–42.

Ware, J. (1987) Providing Education for Children with Profound and Multiple Learning Difficulties: A Survey of Resources and an Analysis of Staff-Pupil Interactions in Special Care Units. Unpublished PhD Thesis, University of London Institute of Education.

Ware, J. (1990) Designing Appropriate Environments for People with Profound and Multiple Learning Difficulties. In Fraser, W. (ed.) *Key Issues in Mental Retardation*. London: Methuen. Proceedings of the Dublin Congress of the IASSID.

Ware, J. (1994) Classroom organisation. In Ware, J. (ed.) *Educating Children with Profound and Multiple Learning Difficulties.* London: David Fulton Publishers.

Ware, J. and Evans, P. (1986) Interactions between profoundly handicapped pupils in a special care class. In Berg, J. and De Jong, J. (eds) *Science and Service in Mental Retardation.* London: Methuen.

Ware, J., Morahan, M., O'Connor, S. and Anderson, M. (1992) Interactions between pupils with severe learning difficulties and non-handicapped peers, *British Journal of Special Education Research*, Section 19(4), 153–8.

Ware, J., Thorpe, P. and Mehigan, P. (forthcoming) Teaching pupils with the most profound general learning disabilities: Workshop Submission for IATSE Conference 2003 'Special Needs: Demands and Delivery'.

Watson, J. S., Hayes, L. and Vietze, P. (1982) Response-contingent stimulation as a treatment for developmental failure in infancy. *Journal of Applied Developmental Psychology* 3, 191–203.

Watson, J. S. and Ramey, C. T. (1972) Reactions to response-contingent stimulation in early infancy. *Merrill-Palmer Quarterly* 18, 219–27.

Wilcox, M. J., Kouri, T. A. and Caswell, S. (1990) Partner sensitivity to communication behavior of young children with developmental disabilities. *Journal of Speech and Hearing Disorders* 55, 679–93.

Wishart, J. (1991) Motivational deficits and their relation to learning difficulties in young children with Down's syndrome. In Watson, J. (ed.) *Innovatory Practice and Severe Learning Difficulties.* Edinburgh: Moray House Publications, Holyrood Road, Edinburgh EH8 8AQ.

Yoder, P. J. (1987) Relationship between degree of infant handicap and clarity of infant cues. *American Journal of Mental Deficiency* 91, 639–41.

Zirpoli, T. and Bell, R. (1987) Unresponsiveness in children with severe disabilities: Potential effects on parent–child interactions. *Exceptional Child* 34 (1), 31–40.

Index

Printed in the United Kingdom
by Lightning Source UK Ltd.
113930UKS00003B/1-82